This book
belongs to the
Second Congregational
Church Library.

I Am a Conductor

Printed in the United States of America

Charles Munch

I Am a Conductor

Translated by Leonard Burkat

New York · Oxford University Press · 1955

Foreword

IT WOULD PROBABLY never have occurred to Charles
Munch, hardly a man of many words, to discuss or
analyze his profession at book length if an enter-
prising publisher had not talked him into it. It is
not unlikely, however, that, having many thoughts
on the subject of the special responsibilities of his
calling, and its privileges too, he was easily drawn
into writing them down. The publisher is the *Édi-
tions du Conquistador* of Paris, which is bringing
out a series personalizing the professions and which
has devoted two books to music. They are *Je suis
compositeur* by Arthur Honegger and *Je suis chef
d'orchestre* by Charles Munch. The emphasis on
the "I" in the titles is, at least in these two cases,
misleading. MM. Honegger and Munch are not to
be classed with those writers who are more than
ready to reveal themselves. Nor are they among
those who with an air of becoming modesty throw
in light anecdotes at their own expense while care-

fully letting the reader gather that their professional abilities have been found irresistible here, there, and everywhere.

It is plain enough that each of these two is completely occupied by his daily tasks. Mr. Munch, like his confrère, has no need to seek more recognition, nor desire to call attention to his successes. He simply takes delight in bringing music to pass in performance. Committed to a text, he has tried to set forth in the light of his own experience what his kind of work involves, what it must encounter, and how it reaches its end—the listening public.

He is describing his profession rather than himself. His account avoids the personal, but inevitably becomes personal on every page. It could not be otherwise, however scrupulously he may reach for generalizations.

When this book appeared in French the audiences of the Boston Symphony Orchestra had had five seasons to become acquainted with Charles Munch. How well can an audience come to know a conductor? Mostly, it sees his back, but, as Mr. Munch points out, seeing is not what counts. It is through the music, which must find its animation in his heart and his mind, that his personal nature is sensed by the audience, sometimes subtly and deeply. Charles Munch upon the platform becomes completely absorbed in Beethoven or Berlioz or Debussy. At the end of the number he defers to

vi

the musicians around him. Bowing is a courtesy to be gone through. The music is the thing. Leaving the stage he makes for home without more ado. No conductor is less inclined to bask in glories accomplished.

So too in his book. He is careless of past achievements, which always make dull reading anyway. To him the present and future are more vital and interesting. From the past comes a memory of friendships, and a fund of experience—a fund from which any conductor (himself included) may profit.

John N. Burk

Contents

Introduction

Toward the end of September 1949, a member of the Boston Symphony Orchestra staff whose work brings him into frequent contact with the conductor went out to a near-by stationery store one afternoon and bought a three-hundred-page blank book, the kind with the black cover and red spine. In a few days the Orchestra's new conductor was to arrive from Paris. Charles Munch had been in Symphony Hall before but only for short visits as a guest conductor. You do not get to know a man very well in three or four weeks but you can learn whether he is interesting or not—and Munch seemed worth starting a new journal for.

After a few weeks the book came out of its place in the bottom right desk drawer less often and soon it lay neglected and forgotten too under an accumulation of memorandum pads and boxes of paper clips. Munch was certainly interesting and in a very distinguished position, but getting to know him came slowly.

He rehearsed his three hours every day, some-times at intermission discussed a current problem for a few minutes with the librarian, the program editor, or the manager—and that was all. His bi-lingual secretary, a musical young Bostonian who had been a clerk in the American Embassy in Paris, delivered an occasional message. Otherwise, there was little communication between Munch and Boston—even with his staff—aside from his ac-tual music-making. He did not hold court in the artists' room after his concerts. By the time the first admirers arrived at his door he was already down-stairs and in his car. He left quietly and alone. In those first years he was 'a stranger and in a strange land.'

* * *

Munch had an uneasy moment not long ago when the owner of the house he has lived in since coming to Boston told him of having received an offer for it from a prospective purchaser, but his fears quickly passed when she said that she enjoyed her short, between-season stays there too much to be willing to part with it. The French have no single word meaning 'home' but they know the sentiment.

The house is a simple and pleasant one, set down in the middle of a plain at the base of a miniature mountain range about twelve miles away from Sym-phony Hall. There is a great lawn behind it, on

xii

which its tenant can practice his golf strokes out of season and where on moonlit winter nights deer can be seen running from one wooded border to another. The countryside is unmistakeably New England with narrow and winding roads that pierce thick woods of birch, elm, oak, and occasional evergreen. To the east and south are the wild hills but just a mile away to the west are the tracks over which the Boston-New York trains pass every hour and a little farther to the north is the marketing center of a suburb whose fortunes are tied to its air-conditioner and paper-box factories. The house is neither clapboard Cape Cod nor red-brick English manor but square and gray stucco with a mansard roof, lacking only a row of poplars to make it seem transplanted from the French countryside. This was once the country home of a noted Episcopal bishop whose daughter now occupies it for only a few weeks late in the spring and again at the end of the summer as she moves between Boston and Bar Harbor. She is pleased to have her house occupied by so important a citizen of Boston as the Conductor of its Orchestra. He is happy to have a house that is a place of refuge in beautiful country and yet is near his work in the city.

Around the first of May every year, the Munch scores and phonograph records go up to the garret storeroom, the piano goes back to the manufacturer's Boston showroom, and seven months' accumulated purchases—from valuable paintings to little American kitchen gadgets—are packed to go back to Paris. *Le patron,* 'the boss,' travels light and by air while the indispensable trio of Alice, Cécile, and Roger, who manage his household, assure the safe transport of all treasured possessions from Boston to Paris.

When his Boston season is over—all the menage returned to France and the bishop's daughter back to Milton—Munch lives in Paris in an apartment that many a museum would envy him.

On a little tree-lined street in the 16th *arrondissement* named for some otherwise forgotten hero or statesman or artist, in one of the great, limestone-faced apartment buildings is the Munch home in Paris. But the concierge does not swing open the handsome iron gate that protects the marbled entrance hall from unwanted, casual callers until the visitor is announced by telephone to the Munch apartment—a condition instituted not in order to create a legend of inaccessibility but to protect the privacy of a man whose position in the world of Paris could be achieved in the United States only by one who combined in a single person the qualities of a national hero and a movie star. (An American friend staying a month in a very small, hundred-year-old, Left-Bank hotel a few years ago found himself suddenly an honored and valued guest on

xiv

the day that Munch drove him back to the hotel and got out of his car to shake hands in the lobby.)

The fourth-floor apartment is reached by a true Paris *ascenseur,* the elevator that ascends with passengers but can only go down empty. Beyond the mirrored entrance hall of the apartment there are many and wonderful things. On the walls, paintings by Brueghel, by Delacroix, by Monet, Sisley, Pissaro. Behind the doors of cabinets that mark the true collector are his drawings and prints, a complete Dürer *Passion,* a choice selection of seventeenth-century Dutch and eighteenth-century French drawings. On shelves and in small glass-covered cases carefully placed where their contents can be most sympathetically lighted and best viewed are the souvenirs of those few free hours that Munch spends in antique shops and second-hand book stores and art galleries. The visitor finds rare relics of the early silversmiths of Munch's native Strasbourg, a fragment of sculpture from Greek antiquity, a precious page of beautifully illuminated manuscript, an old and well-worn pewter mug from which a Norman peasant drank two hundred years ago, or a piece of jade carved by some anonymous Chinese artisan long before Marco Polo first saw his land. Everywhere there are beautiful things—and it is important to add that nowhere is there anything that is not beautiful—selected with care and housed with love.

An observer who had made the rounds of Boston and New York galleries with Munch suddenly found that he had acquired a considerable body of knowledge on the subject of their wares. Munch is an informed collector who usually knows in how many states some beautiful but not very famous print exists, what watermarks to look for in the paper that the masters drew on, the marks to be found on old silver and how to read their complex code language of age, maker, quality, and travel.

As he goes back and forth between Paris and Boston each year, Munch carries with him what he feels he must, but he profits from the best to be found on both sides of the Atlantic. His favorite tailor and shirtmaker are still in Paris but his favorite barber is in Boston.

Americans on their first visits to Europe are often astonished at the things for sale that they don't know how to get at home, but after more than five years Munch has never ceased to wonder at the treasures and jewels still to be found in American shops and galleries that many generations of European collectors have cleared from the shelves of London and Paris dealers. At a cocktail party not long ago, a young banker who is not a collector but knew Munch to be a former violinist and still a violin fancier (among his treasures is the Stradivarius that belonged to the great Belgian

violinist Eugène Ysaÿe) surprised him when he
mentioned that one of the famous Strads had come
down in his family and that it might be offered
for sale, so that it could be used by an artist worthy
of the instrument. There are very few treasures of
this kind still to be disposed of.

Munch is sometimes an 'impulse' or 'occasion'
buyer. The impulse may come after a concert he
thought went particularly well; then he will go to
a silversmith's shop and buy himself a reward. Or
if some matinee should not meet the enormously
high standards dictated by his artistic conscience,
he may buy himself a rare print for consolation.
After a three-month illness some years ago he felic-
itated himself upon his recovery by buying an expensive painting, several Dutch drawings, and, nos-
talgically, some prints by little-known eighteenth-
century artists from Strasbourg.

He does not decide in advance what he must
have and then sit waiting to see the longed-for
treasures listed in dealers' catalogues. When he is
moved to acquire something he goes out to see
what is to be had.

* * *

What a strange accident of history that one of
the most French of French musicians should have
been born a citizen of the German Empire! On
September 26, 1891, when Charles Munch was born
in Strasbourg (Munch taught Bostonians not to

spell it Strassburg), the French border was to the west.

As far back as anyone could remember the men of the Munch family had always been ministers or teachers or organists in the Alsatian churches of the Protestant faith. Charles's father, Ernest, and his uncle, Eugene Munch, grew up in a family of six children at Niederbronn, where their father was a teacher and organist. The two musical boys were thoroughly trained at home. Eugene Munch used to tell his pupil Albert Schweitzer that Bach's *Well-Tempered Clavier* had been his daily bread from infancy. In 1883 the brothers were sent to Berlin to study with August Haupt, the most famous organ virtuoso and teacher of the time.

Returning to Alsace, Eugene became organist of the *Temple Protestant* in Mulhouse (Mülhausen at the time) and then the head of *Chant Sacré,* the city's chief choral society, whose performances of such works as the *Passions* of Bach and the Berlioz *Requiem* he conducted. The first published writing of Albert Schweitzer was a tribute to Eugene Munch, his first organ teacher.

'First of all,' said Schweitzer, 'he tried to bring out the great lines, which he called "the plastic art of organ playing." He delighted in comparing this effort with that of the artist who brings to birth from a block of marble the harmonious forms of

xviii

human beauty. This quality made him majestic as an organ player. . .' *

This was the musician who on his deathbed sang recitatives from Bach's *Passion according to St. Matthew* 'until his dry throat could no longer utter a sound,' reported Schweitzer.

Ernest Munch returned from Berlin to Strasbourg to be organist of Saint William's Church. In December 1884 his petition to the presbytery for permission to form a church choir 'for the purpose of presentation of music in the service of worship' was granted and in Passion Week, 1885, the new chorus of forty singers performed for the first time. Some years later, the church's great Silbermann organ was renovated and the importance of Saint William's in the already busy musical life of Strasbourg was firmly established. This became the place to hear all the important choral literature since Bach, the great masterpieces of the past and the most interesting new music from both sides of the Rhine. One of Ernest Munch's projects, certainly a startling one in its time, was the performance of all the 198 sacred cantatas of J. S. Bach. In addition to singing in the church services, the chorus presented a series of concerts as well—and

* This and other quotations from Albert Schweitzer are taken by permission from *Music in the Life of Albert Schweitzer, with Selections from His Writings,* by Charles R. Joy, New York, Harper & Brothers; Boston, The Beacon Press, 1951.

at all important concerts Eugene came from Mulhouse to play the organ, in the warm and intimate spirit of family collaboration which still continued in the 1930's when Charles Munch used to invite his brother to bring his Strasbourg chorus to Paris to sing with the orchestra he was conducting there then. From 1898 to 1913, after Eugene Munch's death and until his own departure for Africa, the organist of the *Concerts Saint-Guillaume* was Albert Schweitzer.

Ernest, Charles's father, was different from Uncle Eugene. He was less the student, the scholarly searcher, and more the man of temperament and inspiration, the true interpreter and performer. His problems resembled those of performers everywhere. In a heated discussion with church authorities of the deficits incurred by Munch's ambitious and expensive series of orchestra and chorus concerts, Schweitzer, turned publicist, won the day for music when he asked the treasurer, 'Where in Alsace is there a church choir of which the newspapers speak so often?' Ernest was more—and did more—in Strasbourg than just a church organist, and when the combined posts of conductor of the city's orchestra and director of its Conservatory fell vacant, it was generally expected that he would be named to these important and highly prized positions. Dissatisfaction and unhappiness in Strasbourg musical circles were general when the mayor announced the selection of the forty-year-old, Russian-born conductor and composer from Berlin and Munich, Hans Pfitzner, whose fame had already been established by his songs, chamber music, and three successful operas.

'When Munch came to know Pfitzner,' Schweitzer says, 'he felt so profound an admiration for him and his work that he forgave him for having been chosen. As for us, we were happy that Munch had come to know during the weeks of his candidacy in what esteem the people of Strasbourg held him.'

* * *

When Charles Munch was growing up in Strasbourg, it was Pfitzner who supervised his musical studies at the Conservatory. At the same time Munch acquired a thorough classical education at the Gymnase Protestant.

Munch first appeared in public as a performer in 1912, when he and his brother Fritz, who is now Director of the Strasbourg Conservatory and one of France's leading choral conductors, made their debuts as violin and cello soloists—and, according to local historians, with great success.

The musical atmosphere of Strasbourg at the time—like everything else there—was of confused nationality. It is significant that although Ernest and Eugene Munch had gone to Germany to study the organ with the greatest Bach player of the time, the mature Ernest looked for guidance and support not to the *Neue Bachgesellschaft* of Leipzig but to Widor and Bret of the Paris *Société Bach*.

Concert life was busy and active. Von Bülow, Nikisch, Mottl, Strauss, Weingartner, Mahler, Reger, Richter, Massenet, and Walter conducted there during Charles Munch's youth. Busoni, Flesch, Widor, Kreisler, Sarasate, Guilmant, Bauer, Saint-Saëns, Thibaud, Siloti, Schnabel, Ysaÿe, Fauré, Cortot, Dohnanyi, Casals, Zimbalist, and Enesco gave recitals. There was even a traveling Russian chorus, precursor of the Don Cossacks of our day, which passed through Strasbourg, and in 1899 there was a production of *Le Mikado*.

After his Strasbourg debut Munch went off to Paris, seeking a higher schooling under Lucien Capet. He made progress enough to be able to give a recital there but the outbreak of the war found him back at home in Strasbourg, still to be Strassburg for four more years. In 1914 an Alsatian had no choice of nationality. Even Schweitzer, a medical missionary in French Equatorial Africa, was interned as an enemy alien. Munch was a German citizen, and no delicate artist, but a tall, strong, and healthy young man who could not escape being drafted into the German army. Demobilized, he returned home to find employment with a local insurance company as bilingual translator of the fine type in its policies.

But insurance was only a stopgap. Before long Munch was concertmaster of the Strasbourg Orchestra and Professor of Violin at the Conservatory. A few years later he was ready to broaden his horizons, ready to go wherever opportunity called. Had the call come from Paris, he would have gone to the west, but Paris did not yet need Munch. It was to Leipzig he turned and for eight years he sat at the first desk of first violins in the Gewandhaus Orchestra under Wilhelm Furtwängler.

Munch's musical gifts and skills brought him position and importance in the city's musical affairs. He played concertos with the Gewandhaus Orchestra under Furtwängler, and as one of the city's leading violinists participated in all events of musical importance there. But Munch had other ambitions. Perhaps it was the example of Furtwängler, the conductor who was his fast friend and only a few years older and whose reputation had already spread far abroad, that made him want to become a conductor.

Munch left Leipzig in 1932, disturbed by the rising German nationalism and determined to retain his identity as a Frenchman. At the same time, he put down his violin and abandoned for good all concerto playing. He was forty-two years old and burning with ambition to conduct—and to conduct in Paris.

The French capital, at that time, probably had more active orchestras than any other city in the world. Every Sunday afternoon the musical Parisian had a choice of concerts by five different *associations symphoniques*. The most important and the best was the oldest, the *Société des Concerts du Conservatoire,* the Conservatory Concert Society Orchestra. The rest were the Paris Symphony Orchestra and three others known by the names of the nineteenth-century conductors who had established them: the Colonne, Lamoureux, and Pasdeloup Orchestras. In addition there were often many others brought together for special purposes or occasions and those privately maintained like the Siohan or Straram Orchestras. All of them passed from hand to hand—or from baton to baton. Some, like many of Europe's most famous orchestras, could be engaged by anyone who wanted to conduct. Others, following the usual American practice, engaged the most interesting conductors they could find.

Munch began his new career by engaging the Straram Orchestra for a concert on November 1, 1932, and overnight was one of the sought after. When he accepted his second invitation in that same season from the Lamoureux Orchestra, an important critic added prophetically at the end of his enthusiastic review of the concert:

xxiv

'Charles Munch, the young conductor who led this concert, comes, I believe, from Strasbourg. In watching and listening to him, I was moved to predict that he is one of those who, with a special kind of galvanic power, know how to maintain and increase the musical life of a great city.'

Munch was a sudden success, in great demand in Paris and elsewhere. The one thing he wanted to do in the world was conduct and conduct he did wherever he was called. At the *Concerts Siohan,* he played what he pleased—the most difficult and the most radical inventions that interested him —but with the Sunday afternoon *associations symphoniques* the conductor was expected to please the bourgeois rather than arouse them, and this Munch found an unhappy restraint. Characteristically he chose the best but most difficult way out: he started a new orchestra of his own, and with characteristic modesty he called it not *Concerts Munch* but the Paris Philharmonic Orchestra.

This orchestra was much different from the others. Its programs were daring. It played all the new music and all the things its conductor thought should be played—instead of just what sold tickets. And in Paris it was an act of bravery to conduct the Brahms *Requiem* and the Bruckner *Te Deum.* Only a courageous and dedicated young Alsatian would have risked it. He conducted full concert-length works by the most esoteric composers of the day. He lent his orchestra to the International Society for Contemporary Music and conducted the concerts of its Paris Festival. This is the kind of service rendered to the art of music in Paris today only by the government radio orchestras, which alone can indulge a sense of social responsibility. Munch was identified with contemporary music. His work was regarded as the most original and the most interesting. It was this kind of activity that made him an 'original' or a 'character,' that gave him a following of musical bobby-soxers called *les Munchettes,* while at the same time he earned the gratitude and the interest of many forward-looking musicians

Of course programs alone do not make a conducting career—and they did not. Quality remains more important than quantity. His performances, not his repertoire, made him one of the leading new European conductors. He was in great demand everywhere—in London, Vienna, Budapest, Prague.

In the 1930's Virgil Thomson, arriving independently at a specifically American conclusion related to the French critic's 1932 prediction, said that Munch was the kind of conductor who could take over the Boston Symphony Orchestra when the time came for Koussevitzky to retire. It did not happen for about fifteen years but it did happen. From the point of view of American students of the musical scene, Munch's invitation to Boston

marks the high point in his career, but the most
extraordinary single event in his history is really
his appointment to the direction of the *Société des
Concerts* and the professorship of conducting at the
Paris Conservatory when his own conducting career was only five years old. This post was the
most sought after in Paris and represented the
summit of achievement for a French conductor.
It was the 'official' orchestra, the oldest and most
respected. When the directors of the Conservatory
chose Munch for this position, they gave him an
extraordinary vote of confidence.

From 1937 until 1945 Munch remained at his
post in Paris. Early in the war he accepted his first
invitation to conduct in the United States but he
got only as far as Lisbon and then returned to
Paris lest—like several other famous French musicians who sat out the war in New York and Boston—he be unable to return at all.

Munch finds it painful to speak of the Occupation, and his remaining in a semi-official position
in the capital city was misunderstood by a few
Americans when he first came here after the war.
That his record was perfectly clean was abundantly
demonstrated by his frequent participation in the
official celebrations of the Liberation under the
Provisional Government. The most important single event among these was his conducting of a performance of the *Requiem* of Berlioz—composed to

honor the war dead of 115 years earlier—in memory of all those who had given their lives in the Second World War. It was his sincere conviction during the war that he could best serve his countrymen by remaining at his post and doing for them what he knew best how to do. The propriety of his doing so was questioned later by a few of other nationalities but he has always had the full agreement in this of the French.

All during the Occupation his help was very important to the Resistance. For one thing, his substantial earnings helped finance it. For another, his country house was an important way-station on an 'underground railroad' that helped prisoners escaping from the Germans and returned Allied plane crews to England. And he is known to have performed many dangerously kind deeds on behalf of French musicians of the Jewish faith who were deprived of their livelihood and whose lives were often in danger under the German occupation.

The war over, Munch sought a change—relief from the restraints and obligations that had been his daily concern for eight years—and gradually withdrew from responsibility for the *Société des Concerts*. He conducted in Israel and at the festivals in Prague and Edinburgh. In London and Paris he was among the first to conduct for the new postwar high-fidelity recording equipment. He finally made his long delayed visit to the United

xxviii

States, conducting many of the principal orchestras and some of the lesser groups as well. He returned again, repeating his successes, and in 1948 made a transcontinental tour with the French government radio National Orchestra.

The announcement that Serge Koussevitzky was retiring from the musical direction of the Boston Symphony Orchestra and that Munch would be his successor set off a great deal of speculation in musical circles. Boston and New York had known Koussevitzky for twenty-five years. He had a repertoire of enormous range. He was one of the great virtuosos of all time and he had made the orchestra into a virtuoso instrument worthy of himself. He was a master of the classical and romantic repertory; an ardent champion of contemporary music all through his forty years of conducting; so frequent, so sympathetic, and so influential an interpreter of American music during his twenty-five years in Boston that perceptive critics since, in looking back at the music written in this country during that period, have been able to discern a 'Boston Symphony Orchestra style.'

No one really knew how much any of these things dear to the Orchestra's subscribers was going to mean to Charles Munch. He had conducted many different kinds of music during his few brief visits here. We had an idea of what he could do but we did not yet know what a steady diet of Munch would be like. We had seen him and heard him but we did not know him yet.

Munch started cautiously. He understood the importance of Boston—which by French standards should have been considered *en province,* 'in the provinces,' but here is a capital all by itself—the importance of Boston's Orchestra, and the high place it had come to hold in American musical life.

Nothing was more remote from Munch's wish than the sudden creation of an *ancien-nouveau régime* situation. When Munch became Conductor, he did not take from the retiring Koussevitzky direction of the Berkshire Festival and the Berkshire Music Center, the Orchestra's summer festival and summer school which were Koussevitzky's own creation.

But change was inevitable. When the Orchestra was placed in the hands of a new strong man, a thorough musician, an experienced conductor, an artist of firm conviction but of completely different schooling, tradition, ambition, inclination, and attitude toward music, how could there not be change?

There were extra-musical differences too. Munch did not have a twenty-five-year accumulation of convinced admirers. He had to prove himself. And it was some time before he even acquired a few

intimate friends who could be relied upon for ex-
change of honest opinion and original ideas. Un-
critical adulation and exaggerated respectfulness
make life as a man among men difficult to attain
in this conductor-worshipping age.

Little by little, as musicians and music lovers
responded to the new influence at work on them,
changes did take place. Familiar works took on
new aspects. New performances brought new musical principles into action.

Bostonians had become accustomed to thinking
of music in terms of the orchestra. Music had pro-
ceeded orchestrally by steps from color to color but
now it went from phrase to phrase following the
inner 'great line' without regard for the orchestra
as a separate entity. The musical work was ap-
proached in terms of its internal conditions rather
than its orchestral garb.

* * *

Every American is said to have two home towns
—his own and Paris. Munch now has three: Strasbourg and Paris and Boston. Like all good Bostonians he looks on New York as a place providen-
tially placed so near to home that he need spend
no more time there than absolutely necessary. And
then, after coming through the tunnel from Boston's airport and while driving along the Charles
River toward the suburbs, he never fails to say

now, *'C'est agréable, Boston.'* 'It is pleasant to be in Boston.'

It has taken a few years to get to know the flavor of the city and the people. Boston still has its old-world corners, where a European can feel at home: the waterfront, the oldest parts of the city, some still very fashionable and others held to be not so at all. Where small fishing vessels bring their catch to port, where streets are just barely wide enough for an automobile to pass, where there are no neon signs in the shop windows, a newcomer is not always overpowered by America's foreignness, by its constant self-renewal of novelty that is at once the cause and the effect of mass production.

When Munch agreed to conduct a chorus of a thousand students singing Christmas carols on the plaza before Boston's City Hall not long ago, it was not for the simple fun of it or for publicity. It was at once a good deed and an act of gratitude by a new Bostonian.

* * *

The important things to know about Munch are probably these:

He is a man of adventure and action rendered almost immobile, tied down to the demands of one of the most exacting of professions.

He is a libertarian who has arrived at a point of achievement in the freedom-loving world of the arts where he must wield authoritarian powers that would be the envy of many a tyrant.

In a world of complexity, sophistication, vanity, severity, he remains simple, modest, gentle, and warm.

These are the qualities that make him respected by his associates and loved by his friends.

* * *

There is perhaps one anecdote to tell about this conductor of the Boston Symphony Orchestra. One summer day while listening to a report on the foreign students expected to register at the Berkshire Music Center, he heard that there would be 'a boy from Italy and a boy from Israel and a girl from Mexico' and so on, 'And,' Munch added, 'one boy from Alsace.'

Leonard Burkat

I Am a Conductor

1

Prelude on Several Themes

I HAVE BEEN DREAMING of writing this book for more than thirty years—and this is why:

On a wintry night long ago I wandered out into the snow-covered streets of Strasbourg half drunk with music and carried away with admiration for a conductor who had just revealed a Brahms symphony to me. As I made my way through the crowd leaving the hall, I picked up a scrap of conversation that I have never been able to forget.

'Lovely concert,' murmured a disagreeable voice.

'Bah,' said a presumptuous person whose conviction froze me to the spot. 'The orchestra is fine but I wonder why we must always have a conductor in front of it.'

3

'That's exactly what I was asking myself all through the Brahms symphony,' said the disagreeable voice with a little laugh of self-satisfaction.

At this point I could scarcely contain my mad desire to tell the disagreeable lady and the presumptuous gentleman in two plain words to be still. Now at last I shall talk back to them—at greater length and without fear of interruption.

How many thousands of things about conducting they were unaware of. That it is not a profession at all but a sacred calling, sometimes a priesthood, and often even a disease—a disease from which the only escape is death. That fifteen years of work and study do not make a conductor of a man if he is not possessed by an inner exaltation, an all-consuming flame, and a magnetism that can bewitch both the musicians of his orchestra and the audience come to hear his music-making.

* * *

The French word for conductor, *chef d'orchestre,* 'orchestra chief,' connotes command, but the conductor's problem is not so much the command itself as its communication. His medium is not speech but gesture, posture, telepathy, and an irresistibly keen radiation.

Standing on the podium, at the instant when his hand marks the first beat of a symphony by Beethoven or Brahms, the conductor is the cynosure of all eyes, the hearth to which thou-

4

sands have come for warmth and light. He can only live, let his heart beat, his soul vibrate, and his emotions sing.

* * *

Scrupulously and conscientiously the conductor analyzes the themes, the harmonies, and the orchestration of his scores. Laboriously and patiently he rehearses his program four or five times. All his intelligence and all his senses are always at the service of his art. Yet one day he is the public's darling and the next he is out of grace.

Why? Who is to blame? Conductor, orchestra, or public? Hans von Bülow used to say that there are no bad orchestras, only bad conductors. I can add that there is no bad public. The total responsibility is the conductor's.

No one is more exposed to criticism. The mechanical perfection of a violinist's technique can be admired complacently but a conductor can be judged only in terms of the artistic function he performs and the emotions he arouses.

The fraction of the public whose sympathies can be moved by a good view of a handsome profile or by a demonstration of the conductor's courage in attacking trombones, the few hearts that can be captured by a well-cut jacket are negligible. The conductor need not dramatize his function. The best part of the audience has come to listen,

5

to hear music it loves or at least finds interesting—not to look.

* * *

I urge every apprentice to imbue himself early with a sense of the conductor's responsibility. For a long time everything has been so ordered as to make it difficult to forget.

You perch on a pedestal in the middle of a battlefield. You are Saint Sebastian exposed to the Roman arrows. You are Joan of Arc ready to burn at the stake for what you love. If even after forty years of conducting you are still struck to the heart before every concert by fear and panic that overwhelm you with the strength of a tidal wave, if you feel this formidable transport of anguish still more intensely each time, you are still making progress and every time you conduct you will understand your mission a little better.

There are many reasons for your anguish. It is you who must breathe life into the score. It is you and you alone who must expose it to the understanding, reveal the hidden jewel to the sun at the most flattering angles. Your task is one of setting and is as delicate as the film director's, measuring out light and dark, sharp images and blurred, groping toward the projection of an ideal that does not exist in real life.

It is not easy.

6

Your thought, your communication must radiate with such force that your orchestra feel simultaneously the same wishes and desires as you and cannot refrain from expressing them. You must substitute your will for theirs.

The collective conscience of a hundred musicians is no light burden. Think for a moment of what it would mean to a pianist if by some miracle every key of his instrument should suddenly become a living thing. A friend of mine, a musician in the *Orchestre de la Suisse romande,* once said to me, 'When every member of the orchestra feels that you are conducting for him alone, you are conducting well.' He gave me food for thought.

* * *

A conductor's effectiveness is limited if he cannot depend to some degree on a magic emanation from his person. Some have only to make their appearance. Even before they have raised a hand for attention, the atmosphere changes. Their simple presence is stirring, charges the air. You feel that some rare phenomenon is about to take place. Other conductors walk on the stage and nothing happens—before, during, or after the concert.

Sometimes in thinking about this I have sought a definition of 'conductor.' Is his first function to co-ordinate the forces he leads? Or is it more important to impose a common aesthetic on musicians whose temperaments may oppose or neutralize one another? Should he take the position of the musical scholar striving to rediscover the traditions, the tempi, and the nuances that Mozart himself would have sought in performing *The Marriage of Figaro*? Or should he be the kind of specialist who spends hours at his desk over a single score, scrutinizing and searching for riches and beauties and traps, for sections and outlines? The conductor must be all these and it makes no difference which of them he becomes first if he has the courage and patience to conquer in the silence of his study all the technical difficulties that must be surmounted and made to pass unnoticed on the evening of the concert.

There are conductors who know their business thoroughly and still never arouse any enthusiasm. Any definition of conducting that takes into account only knowledge and professional skill will be found sadly lacking. What is still missing?

I believe that every human being endowed with intelligence, memory, and strength of character bears within him a little of the supernatural as well. The highest purpose of the conductor is to release this superhuman potential in every one of his musicians. The rest is corollary, indispensable certainly, but only enough to make a professional conductor—not the combined servant and eloquent lover that music demands.

The conductor's feelings should be the mirror

8

in which music sees her own reflection, as nature is reflected in the eye of the painter. When Renoir painted a landscape, he revealed its warmth, its mystery, its poetry. When some Sunday dauber attacks the same subject, a soulless stereotype appears on his canvas, revealing none of the scene's secrets. In the same way, a poor conductor may dry up and debase music in which others discover nobility and expressions of human joy or sadness or love.

Music is an art that expresses the inexpressible. It rises far above what words can mean or the intelligence define. Its domain is the imponderable and impalpable land of the unconscious. Man's right to speak this language is for me the most precious gift that has been bestowed upon us. And we have no right to misuse it.

Whenever I am about to conduct a concert, at the moment when the musicians are holding their breath and the bows are held a fraction of an inch in the air above the strings, at that moment of infinite silence before the first note is heard, all these thoughts run through my mind—just as all your life is said to pass in a flash before your eyes at the moment of death.

Let no one be astonished then that I consider my work a priesthood, not a profession. It is not too strong a word. And like all sacred callings, that

9

of the conductor supposes a total self-renunciation and a profound humility.

I have chosen to point out the nobility of our mission rather than the everyday professional problems but before the conductor deserves the right to mount his stand and there to contemplate his hundred musicians and the thousand-headed Hydra called the public, he must work indefatigably. He must learn what the foils are and how to overcome them.

* * *

'To command well, you must know how to obey.' This one, like all the old sayings, contains a great truth.

How many pianists and violinists and other instrumentalists of all kinds vegetating in the conservatories console themselves with 'If I do not succeed at my instrument, I can become a conductor.' In truth they sometimes do. But they soon discover that with less than exceptional natural gifts, a conductor must acquire a technique that cannot be improvised.

Of all the different kinds of musical performance none looks easier than conducting. We even have child prodigies now, some of whom go so far as to found their glory—and their publicity—on the fact that they do not know how to read music. Does this mean that it is really unnecessary, perhaps even useless, for conductors to know how to read scores? You can be sure that the musicians of any major orchestra will come out together at the end of a Beethoven symphony—even though the conductor may still have a little way to go. Of course such a performance will not be regarded as a great interpretation or applauded as such. But suppose that a new work is having its first performance. How will the orchestra grope its way through the intricate maze of complex rhythms and harmonies without the help of an enlightened guide?

Any musician worthy of the name may presume to conduct an orchestra but few have pierced the veil hiding the secrets of this musical métier that is apparently the easiest but is in fact the most difficult. I know what Richard Strauss meant when he said, 'Even if you know that conducting is difficult, you must be a seventy-year-old conductor to understand just how difficult it is.'

The public cannot imagine the conductor's ant-like labors, the obligations he accepts and the discipline he imposes on himself. He has not the right to be unacquainted with any potential of any orchestral instrument or to underestimate the latest discoveries of contemporary composers. He must be equally proficient at discerning bayonet thrusts in Beethoven's Fifth and Hindu rhythms in Messiaen's scores. He has not the right to disregard traditions but it is his duty to diagnose their faults of logic—for blindly followed tradition may be treason. He has not the right to let a copyist's error slip by in the musicians' parts. He has not the right to let an orchestra acquire habits or fall into dry routine. He has not the right to be inattentive for a single second or to be sleepy the night before a rehearsal if he has not finished studying his scores, or to have a stomach-ache on the evening of a concert, or to rest on his laurels the next day believing he has really arrived because the audience demanded encores of the *Meistersinger* Overture or *La Valse* or some other work of which he has made a profitable specialty. He has only the right to be talented, the right to love music and conducting, and the duty to consider every performance a combat of uncertain outcome.

Every concert requires an unbelievable outlay of intellectual, nervous, and physical strength. You give a little of your life with each one but you must be cold-blooded enough to know that you might have given more.

Your fifteen years of study and all your natural gifts are still not enough. It takes work to make a conductor. You must work from the day you first walk through the conservatory door to the night when, exhausted, you conduct the last concert of your career.

* * *

Is it paradoxical to assert that my duties and disappointments rather than my successes are the basis of my infinite love for my work? This unremitting toil to which I have bound myself for so long, all the manuscripts I have sat bent over until dawn, all the orchestras whose enthusiasm I have had to arouse even during wartime rehearsals in halls invaded by freezing-cold morning fogs, all these have taught me a lesson in compassion.

My profession gives me opportunity for intense self-expression and freedom for any flight of the imagination. To a reserved, withdrawn, and timid person it offers the chance to realize his dreams in sound. Those who listen may find different things in these sounds—expression of their own desires, their own emotions, their own thoughts. A conductor, in giving a faithful reproduction and exact translation of the written notes, can re-create the thought and emotion of an unknown person—the composer—which can sometimes be a transfiguring experience.

* * *

I am often asked both in France and the United States, 'How do you become a conductor?' Heaven knows that it takes enthusiasm, love, patience, and work.

Aside from this, it is of course obvious that there are various more or less efficient ways of developing innate gifts. Since the human element is so important here, I think that there is no one infallible recipe. Every budding conductor is a special case.

One will be drawn to contemporary music, another to the romantic. A third will blossom only in demonstrating the mechanics of *The Art of the Fugue* and will have no understanding at all of the spirit of Schumann. Take your choice. I believe a universal talent to be the rarest exception. Some have built their entire careers on a dozen scores—and not from laziness but humble prudence.

Before I tell you how I happened to become a conductor, I must warn you that luck had a great deal to do with it. On the strength of having wished to conduct an orchestra, I have conducted a hundred. But I have worked too and I work still. I reflect. I suffer my qualms. I sometimes even return, incognito, to the classroom.

My only reason for writing this book is so that future conductors who have faith and who wish to serve music rather than be served by it may profit from my experience. If at the same time I explain what it means to be a conductor, then I shall have handed on the key to the temple of the gods of music, exacting gods whom it is sacrilege to disappoint.

2

Years of Apprenticeship

EVERYONE KNOWS the musician's autobiography that begins 'I have been listening to music since the day I was born. My father played the clarinet. At an early age my brothers and sister and I formed a string quartet and we spent our school vacations deciphering the classical masterpieces of the repertoire, the works of Haydn, Mozart, and Beethoven.' Mine is not much different.

I was born in Strasbourg, where music has always been important and still is. Before the Bach cult had rediscovered and universally glorified the great Johann Sebastian, his cantatas and passions were sung in Strasbourg at the *Concerts Saint-Guillaume,* of which my father was the founder.

It seems that I sang well as a little boy, so well that one Sunday at Christmas I was asked to sing a solo during the service, accompanied at the organ by my father. But when the time came, I was paralysed with fright, incapable of making a sound. It was a dreadful experience. To this day I have been unable to forget the nightmare of that sad debut. I was still very young when my father let me join his chorus and it was in choral singing that I learned *solfège* and the rudiments of music unawares.

All this was good schooling. Albert Schweitzer was our organist. Charles-Marie Widor and Gustave Bret, the founders of the Paris Bach Society, used to come to our concerts. Sometimes Widor played one of his great symphonies for organ and orchestra under my father's direction.

I used to attend their rehearsals and afterward listen to these great men argue bitterly about details of interpretation. Their debate sometimes took so violent a turn that my mother had to run to the protection of her furniture. The scarcity of dynamic indications in seventeenth- and eighteenth-century scores occasioned passionate controversy. The opinions of the most important musicologists were passed in review, the solutions of other conductors considered, and finally all reasoning was abandoned and each spoke from his heart

16

alone. It was from this, I believe, that I really learned to *love* music.

My father could not imagine his children being anything but musicians. As soon as I learned to read music and to sing pretty nearly in tune, I was given a manual of harmony and a treatise on counterpoint and was assigned to a teacher as severe as he was wise, Charles-Marie Erb. At the same time I studied the violin with Nast at the Strasbourg Conservatory and for experience played on the last stand of second violins in my father's orchestra. I learned a great deal from this observation post.

* * *

After the absorption of Alsace by the German Empire in 1871, Strasbourg had become a strategic center of Franco-German artistic rivalry. The most important conductors of the time took turns before our orchestra. Nikisch had hardly quieted the last shudder of a Brahms symphony when Colonne or Pierné counterattacked with Berlioz or the latest works of the new French school that was then so rich and productive.

I remember best a concert conducted by Vincent d'Indy, a musician who could be stubborn and charming, technician and poet at the same time. After his three hours of hard work in rehearsal he liked to go walking and I was his guide through old Strasbourg. I considered myself well compensated for my services when on concert night he

17

allowed me to carry his scores to the hall. And then when he got back to Paris, this exalted gentleman found time to send me a note of thanks in his own fine hand. It was 1905. I was fourteen years old.

* * *

By the age of six I had begun to try my hand at the organ, to hammer on the piano and scratch a little on the violin. I loved the organ and piano but my start on the violin was painful—which did not prevent me from becoming a violinist. Once I was given a trumpet as a gift. It was in the country, near Niederbronn, where we used to spend our vacations at my grandfather's house. After a few walks in the woods with it I finally managed to make some almost coherent sounds but in a while the trumpet was so battered that it was barely worth keeping around the house. I used to find the tone of the clarinet infinitely seductive in those days but I could never collect enough money to buy one. The day will come, I hope. . .

* * *

The organ was my first orchestra. If you have never played the organ, you have never known the joy of feeling yourself music's master, sovereign of all the gamut of sounds and sonorities. Before those keyboards and pedals and the palette of stops, I felt almost like a demigod, holding in my hands the reins that controlled the musical universe.

18

I played well enough to be able to take my father's place in church sometimes and this was my great joy. Walking along the river to St. William's, opening the little door to the organ with a big old key, looking over the day's hymns lest I forget the repeats, finding a prelude in a good key in order to avoid a difficult modulation, choosing a gay piece for a wedding or a sad one for a funeral, not falling asleep during the sermon, sometimes improvising a little in the pastor's favorite style, not playing a long recessional because it would annoy the sexton—all this filled me with pride.

* * *

Inflated pride persuaded me that heaven had withheld no gift, but I learned. I began to compose. I wrote music as others at the same age write sonnets during algebra class. My music teacher had briefly explained a few of the problems but had not considered it necessary that I have command of any more complex form than the minuet. But my visions were of greater import, grander and nobler.

Here's the whole story: I am the composer of a sonatina, a few songs (what musician has not written a few songs?), and the beginning of a string quartet. Since I do not believe in unrecognized genius and since no one has ever performed my sonatina in public, I am forced to conclude that my mission as a composer was a delusion. And my quartet remains unfinished.

I did learn something from my spatterings on music paper. I have an idea of the composer's compulsions. Knowing what difficulties he has had to overcome, I can admire his skill and his genius with fuller understanding.

*　*　*

I was a violinist first of all and I could put my instrument aside only to take up my school books—for I still had my diploma to earn. When I finally got it, I left for Paris firm in my intention of becoming a violin virtuoso under the tutelage of the famous Lucien Capet.

I don't know yet why I undertook the study of medicine at the same time. To what advantage I might have used those hours I spent at the medical school, hours I contrived so ingeniously to shorten that in the eyes of Aesculapius I was soon nothing but a name on the University rolls.

*　*　*

1914-1918, the war. I returned to Strasbourg on the last train to cross the blue ridge of the Vosges. After four years far from music the best situation I could find was an extremely modest one with the Rhine and Moselle Insurance Company.

Little by little, in the evenings, I began to play the violin again. I rented an old piano that was to sound its last chords at my hands. Alone in my room I satisfied my hunger for music. My appetite for it grew daily and in a little while my usefulness to the insurance business was found to be such that the company could painlessly dispense with my services.

By a stroke of good fortune a vacancy occurred in the violin section of the Strasbourg orchestra just a few weeks later. Guy Ropartz, the Director of the Conservatory, presided over an open competition for the place and Fortune smiled on me. I was chosen to bear the title of Assistant Concertmaster. At the same time as I got my first job, I won the affection of Ropartz, who was to be a second father to me, my counselor and guide. If it were not for him I might now be concertmaster in Strasbourg.

A place on the Conservatory faculty went with my new post in the orchestra. Playing the symphonic repertoire under Ropartz, playing French and German operas under Paul Bastide, and giving lessons all taught me a great deal.

I lived the calm but ardent life of the provincial musician whose fame is unlikely to cross any borders. I had taken almost every course offered at the Conservatory except orchestra conducting but the idea that I would one day take my turn at their head and be a leader among my comrades was always in the back of my mind. I watched Bastide and Ropartz as an entomologist watches insects. All their gestures were soon so familiar to me that I could execute them automatically before I ever had occasion to use them. When I did not have to play, I used to sit in a corner of the hall with the score or try to get an idea of the techniques of the other instruments.

* * *

One fine morning I learned through the kindness of the *Thomascantor* Karl Straube that the place of concertmaster in the Leipzig orchestra was vacant. Without a moment's hesitation, Ropartz allowed me to try my luck and offered me a year's leave. I came out of this contest in first place. Seeing my enthusiasm for my work, Ropartz later extended my leave for two more years. I shall never be able to thank him enough.

Every Sunday morning, I played in the chamber orchestra that accompanied Bach cantatas in the *Thomaskirche,* the Leipzig church where Bach himself had been Cantor. One Saturday afternoon Cantor Straube sprained his ankle and asked the organist to conduct for him on the following morning. The organist preferred not to and Straube asked me. With the audacity of youth I accepted immediately. I studied the score all night and conducted it the next morning. 'It went beautifully,' I wrote home proudly to my parents, 'and it was a wonderful experience. My colleagues were wide-eyed!'

It was in Leipzig too that I had my second experience in conducting. It was a kind of 'historical

22

concert' conducted by the concertmaster from his place in the orchestra as Ferdinand David had done about a hundred years before. This concert was the decisive event for me. I decided to give up the violin and try my luck as a conductor.

* * *

In 1932 historic events persuaded me to leave Germany for good. I passed through Strasbourg but there was no longer anything for me to do there. Not wishing to abuse his kindness, I had sent my resignation to Ropartz long before.

I entered Paris by the same *Gare de l'Est* as twenty years before—almost to the day—rich in nothing but hope. This time I had different ambitions, a little more experience, and a burning desire to make it known *urbi et orbi* that my destiny as a conductor was written in the stars.

The public found this a less pressing matter than I did. Assembling all my financial resources, I engaged the Straram Orchestra, which had a world-wide reputation at the time as a champion of new music. I cannot honestly say that I conducted the orchestra for I was fully occupied with allaying the fear that paralysed me. I walked on the stage with the feeling that I was floating through a heavy fog. My legs felt no weight. I was a stranger to the laws of gravity. I floated through a dream-world where all was *not* rosy and I conducted like an automaton. My sympathetic audience mistook my panic for inspiration. Do not ask me whether it was a good concert. I heard nothing and saw nothing. I left the hall as one leaves a hospital after a long illness. But I cut my convalescence short. When summer came, I left for Biarritz to conduct the season there. Later I was invited to conduct the Lamoureux Orchestra.

I visited Paul Bastide often during this time and profited greatly from his advice. I told him my troubles, let him know my doubts, and discussed countless problems with him. He came to my concerts and then with extraordinary perception took up one by one and measure by measure the mistakes I had made. It was still a time of working and learning.

I became friendly with Honegger, Roussel, and Poulenc and often played their works at the concerts of the Paris Philharmonic Orchestra, which I conducted for three years. Contemporary music attracted me more and more as the living expression of the aspirations and tastes of our own times. Is not this the music we should understand best?

1937 . . . a miracle. Upon the resignation of Philippe Gaubert the *Société des Concerts du Conservatoire* found itself without a regular conductor. The orchestra board engaged me for a few concerts and then asked that I consider myself a candidate for the vacant post—which I should never have had the courage to do on my own initiative.

So one fine day I found my name graven in letters of gold on the marble plaque at the entrance to the old Conservatory where the concerts of the *Société* then took place. I conducted this marvelous orchestra every Sunday until 1945, striving at every concert to bring still more thought, more care, more passion to bear on the practice of my art.

During the four terrible years of German occupation my role was to help saddened souls escape to happier worlds. I worked at it with an ardor that was multiplied a thousandfold by the pain of seeing my country gagged, enchained, and murdered. No material force could ever break the heart of music.

The war prevented me from accepting my first invitation to the United States, but in 1946 I conducted American orchestras from New York to Los Angeles and from Chicago to Houston. In 1948 I traveled across the American continent again with the *Orchestre national de la radiodiffusion française*. Then in 1949 the Boston Symphony Orchestra invited me to take the place of Serge Koussevitzky, who was retiring after twenty-five seasons at its head.

* * *

If I stop this chapter here, it is not because my apprenticeship is over. Working stops when learning stops. But the American adventure deserves a longer account at another time.

3

Becoming a Conductor

Now THAT YOU KNOW how I became a conductor, take this advice: Don't do it my way. Chance, happy chance has had a big part in my career but it is better to start out with a detailed battle plan rather than trust too much to luck—except of course that you must be ready to take advantage of it when you can. And bear in mind besides that these days, when everything is organized, systematized, and standardized, conducting careers are not made by chance.

In France, in the United States, and everywhere there is a lot of machinery to set in motion if you want to become the conductor of a symphony or-

chestra. When you have passed through this con-
ductor-making machine, you find that there is a
bigger market for your talents than there was for
those of my generation. In France the national
radio is a big help. Everywhere there are radio and
television, opera, ballet and theatrical companies,
and many more. The interest of a good manager
can be effective and is sometimes even indispensable, but there are no employment agencies in our
field yet.

In spite of all the new opportunities, there are
no more great conductors in the world than there
used to be. I find this a cheering phenomenon.
Does it not prove that talent and innate gifts must
still precede glory and renown?

* * *

I should really have liked to be a stage director
and designer, to see living actors in their roles, to
be able to direct them, control their movements
and the intensity of their emotions. A musician
can understand perfectly the profound changes in
characterization that take place on a level where
words can no longer express emotions. There,
where subconscious and dream begin, the domain
of the musician begins.

* * *

Having 'conductor' printed on your card will
not make you one. You must earn the right to call

yourself a conductor and you can do so only by proving yourself an artist.

One of the reasons that conducting is difficult is that it presupposes an enormous body of theoretical and technical knowledge. Since you conduct all the instruments, you must know them all. You conduct music with which you have no previous acquaintance—and there is even a time when Beethoven's Fifth is a first performance for you—so you must be able to identify yourself with the composer and rediscover for yourself his intentions and his state of mind. You must make a thorough study of the means of communication between conductor and orchestra. And especially because music is getting more complicated every day, you must not omit the smallest particle of musical knowledge from your education.

I think that thorough acquaintance with an orchestral instrument is of the greatest importance and I am convinced that mastery of one of the strings is the most profitable. The strings are the foundation of the orchestra and it is important to know exactly what you can expect them to do. In times gone by, most conductors had been violinists. By tradition, the leader of the first violins took the conductor's place when necessary.

Playing an instrument lets you in on the inside. Nikisch was a violinist and Toscanini a cellist. It is the best way of discovering the problems that

28

face the musician. They are at worst a mere shadow of the conductor's but you will be on the right track.

You can tell at a glance and sometimes from a single chord whether the conductor knows all the subtleties of the strings. Has he arranged the bowings so that every note will have the special quality he desires? He will not really know what to expect if he has not tried them himself. At the same time, it is important to avoid seeming to play an imaginary violin while conducting. An allusive gesture may sometimes be necessary but systematic mimicry complicates the musicians' task. The signs they need are at once precise and evocative.

It is good to know the wind instruments too— both wood and brass—to familiarize yourself with their timbres and to know their coefficients of virtuosity. The problem of attack varies a great deal from one to another, from horn to oboe, for example. You don't give trombone and flute the same kind of send-off. The musicians have breaths to take and motions to make that are measured in tiny fractions of a second—precious fractions when you need an attack in perfect unison. You must know either instinctively or from experience the precise moment at which to bring each one into play.

Thorough study of a good treatise on instrumentation is indispensable. Look at Gevaert or Widor or Berlioz-Strauss, at Forsyth or Piston.

It is impossible to know how to play every instrument and the best way to get acquainted with them is still to sit with a score in your lap at every orchestral performance you attend, following the phrases of piccolo or trombone or oboe. In Paris it is especially interesting to attend the annual competitions at the Conservatory. When you have heard thirty clarinetists play a *Caprice* composed especially to test and show every quality of instrument and player, you will not soon forget what the clarinet sounds like and what it can do.

And why not attend a conservatory class as an auditor from time to time? There are always discoveries still to be made. I proved it to myself during my 1953 vacation when I attended Passerone's percussion classes and Sabaritch's in trumpet at the Paris Conservatory.

* * *

And then there is the music—the music written on twenty-four lines or more that you must be able to read simultaneously. If only for safety's sake, you should have complete command of harmony and counterpoint. Educate your ear, for you work with your ears even more than with your arms. How many times have I said at rehearsal, 'Listen to what the others are doing, gentlemen. Listen to what is going on around you. It will make

30

the rehearsal seem shorter and more interesting and everything will sound better.'

The study of *solfège*, which is essential to the practice of our art, is sometimes treated lightly in the conservatories, but it is more important today than ever. Twelve-tone music and other kinds of modern harmony are full of traps for ill-trained ears.

The knowledge of figured bass, harmony and counterpoint, the ability to play a Bach choral in four different clefs, all this helps the conductor to analyze a score, see how its gears mesh and what makes it tick, helps him to understand the structure and its delicate elements of balance.

It is easy to tell what a chord is in a piece of piano music. With a full orchestra score your eyes and ears must be thoroughly trained. Copying orchestra scores is an excellent exercise. There is nothing more tedious—or more effective. You inscribe the notes on paper and the sounds in your mind at the same time. As the ink dries a kind of auditory crystallization takes place and with a little practice you 'hear' what you write more distinctly than when just reading notes. You soon find that you are no longer content with simply running your eyes over a score. You can no longer let it keep any secret from you.

I also recommend that you try orchestrating. It is much more satisfying than just copying. Take any song or sonata, or orchestrate the piano reduction of a symphony and compare your work with the composer's original. You will be surprised at the differences.

A good memory is one of the conductor's trumps. Studying, copying, orchestrating sharpen the visual memory of the score page. Every conductor should be naturally endowed with *la mémoire sonore* as well, the aural memory, the ability to remember and recognize sounds, to retain in the mind a sonorous image of things heard as he might the visual image of things seen. You must be able to hear more than others do, to remember what you have heard, to recognize it when you hear it again, and to recall at will any aural impression.

* * *

For two years I had charge of the conducting class at the Paris Conservatory and, just as when I had taught violin at Strasbourg, I learned a great deal. Our first step in studying a symphonic movement was to analyze its construction, break it down into phrases to see how it was put together. Take the opening of the *Eroica,* for example. The first two measures are two chords. Then there is a twelve-measure period that can be broken down into three four-measure phrases. You know a great deal about a piece of music when you know where every phrase starts and stops.

Then after a harmonic analysis of the structure

one student played the score at the piano while another stood up and conducted. I used to ask that he conduct simply and, above all, clearly. I did not permit conducting without a baton, which has unhappily become fashionable. It is a bad habit, in my opinion, that creates difficulties for the musicians. I am sure that anyone who has ever played in a professional orchestra will agree with me. I always consider the baton an extension of the body, magnifying every movement of arm and hand in space. The essential thing is perfect clarity of gesture, which is becoming more difficult and more important every day because of the metrical complexity often found in modern music.

The right arm beats the meter, the left indicates the nuances. The first is reason's, the second the heart's, and the right hand must always know what the left is doing. The conductor's aim is perfect coordination of gesture with complete independence of the arms, so that one side will not contradict the other.

I did not require my pupils to learn their scores by heart. As Reynaldo Hahn said, 'You go to concerts to admire the music, not the conductor's feats of memory.' I have seen some of the greatest memory-acrobats make catastrophically sad mistakes. It is especially dangerous to conduct accompaniments by heart. I know that it always makes soloists nervous.

Finally, it is not wise to send young conductors out to do battle without preparation by an acute observer whose principal purpose has been to correct their every motion, suppress their every superfluous gesture, refine their styles. The teacher shows his students all the dangers but their own experience will teach them best how to avoid them. And on the day when they can at last stand up in front of real, live orchestras, the young conductors will be on their way.

* * *

Does the public suspect the physical strain of conducting a two-hour concert? The conductor, by definition inspired and poetical, must have unusual nervous and muscular equipment. He must be as exact and expressive near the end of his labors as at the beginning. This is one of the athletic aspects of conducting that has convinced me of the importance of gymnastics in our work. Gymnastics help attain a higher physical discipline, ease of movement, and independence of the arms. It teaches how to conserve energy and to overcome fatigue.

* * *

Then the day comes when the student leaves the Conservatory. He has to earn his living but there is small likelihood that an orchestra will come to seek his services. And happily so, for his apprenticeship is only beginning. The new conducting

34

diploma is like a new driving license. It is better not to use it on the super-highways without some more practice. And for this, the young conductor must unhesitatingly seek out a post with an orchestra, if only a modest post as a player. From his place there let him watch the masters of his profession at work. Let him watch his neighbors, his comrades, and learn to know an orchestra's reactions. An orchestra is a battalion and you must penetrate the depths of its mind before presuming to command it.

Finally the hour will strike when he too can take control. Let him not believe that his studies are over now. A conductor's life is a perpetual renewal of learning.

In this connection I have never forgotten an experience I had once with Toscanini. I was already conducting when he came to Paris once for a series of concerts. Thinking that nothing could be more instructive, I asked the orchestra manager's permission to play with the first violins. An extra chair was put on the stage for me behind the usual last stand, but my extra violin part did not have the same bowings as the others. Toscanini noticed immediately that my bow went down when the others went up and told me so. I felt that his eyes never left me throughout the rest of the session. Imagine my surprise, on meeting him again in New York

35

many years later, at his perfect recollection of the incident.

Throughout our careers we must know how to take advantage of every opportunity offered us. We never finish learning!

4

Making the Program

THE PROGRAM—the conductor's first pre-concert
care and a complicated one with so many different
elements to consider.

First there are your personal preferences. Play
the music you love but avoid building all your
career on two or three programs that may seem to
assure success but will surely render no service to
the art of music. Do not risk falling into the quick-
sand of routine. You will be working less hard,
which is fatal. There is no reputation that can resist this kind of spreading mediocrity.

Many conductors have 'war-horses' that they ride
at certain times but if they wish to travel far they

must spare their mounts. Others pass themselves off as specialists in some particular piece or in one composer. Such conductors have never inspired anything in me but suspicion.

* * *

You must take into account the taste and the wishes of the public—but only up to a certain point. The music, the interpreter, and the public form a tri-partite entity in which each factor is indispensable to the others. Each has its rights and its duties.

The public comes to concerts to hear good performances of beautiful music just as it goes to museums to look at beautiful pictures or statues. It comes to be enriched, instructed, fortified. It does not come to criticize. It comes to take its place in the trinity with the composer and the performer. I am speaking of course of a 'good' public, which listens thoughtfully and receptively to good music and good interpreters.

We know that music lovers all over the world want to hear the Beethoven symphonies but we limit the field of our activities and in fact betray our art if we do not show music's many other aspects.

Above all, never attempt to flatter and indulge the public. Do not play a Sibelius symphony for a Finnish audience just because you know they like it. Because they like it, they know it, and knowing it, they will never forgive your attempted flattery if your interpretation is not of the best.

* * *

If you make your programs too long, you will weary your audience. Music requires a state of high nervous tension on the part of both listener and performer. Don't overstrain it. A concert should not ordinarily have much more than seventy-five minutes of music if you do not want to hear the rustling of inattention or the noise of seats slamming behind you.

It is difficult to give an example of a typical program. Here is one scheme among many that seem reasonable to me:

1. A classical symphony or a baroque concerto grosso or an overture.

2. A difficult work. This is the place for Berg or Bartók.

3. A big symphony.

First we prepare the terrain and sharpen the receptivity. Then we can try to make the public love music whose tartness may still be disturbing. Finally, the classical, rich and solid, relaxes the atmosphere.

Build the program in such a way as to keep audience attention without a moment's waning. There are two ways to do it. First, select and perform the works in order of increasing tension. Second, give an impression of variety by juxtaposing works of very different periods, styles, or characters.

Consider the orchestra too when you make your program. Musicians do not have the same instincts, reactions, or habits all over the world. Where you do not have many rehearsals, it is wise not to play works completely unfamiliar to the orchestra, or, more properly, in a style or spirit totally strange to it.

The first principle is to choose works that suit your temperament and the orchestra's and the public's all at the same time. This is a difficult but necessary condition, although still not enough by itself for a true musical communion.

* * *

The custom of putting the soloist, if there is one, at the end of the program has been spreading from the United States. It is a practice that I do not much favor for it breaks what should be the unity of a concert into two disparate halves. I do not consider it wise to present the soloist in a kind of side show, for it gives the public the impression that the rest of the concert is really only a framework for the freak. Nor do I care for the resemblance to the music-hall system in which the time is simply filled in with less brilliant acts until the appearance at the end of the star acrobat everyone has been waiting for.

And incidentally I think that 'evenings' and 'fes-

40

tivals' of a single composer are very much overdone these days. It is a program-making formula that I avoid. I do not like to be classified and labeled.

Music should be treated chivalrously, not put on parade.

* * *

There are many other burdens on your conscience at the moment of fixing on a program. Must you play contemporary music? I agree with this aphorism of Saint-Saëns: 'The two kinds of music are not the contemporary and the other kind but the good and the other.' Of course the knowledge that Beethoven's symphonies are good does not require you to measure all others by his. But having accepted the principle, when you find good contemporary music, can you play it without risk?

This is really no problem. It is proper to play some at every concert but with moderation, lest the public be discouraged. Nothing does modern music a greater disservice than dissociating it from the rest of the repertoire. Doing so is an imposition that may not be borne with good will, for it demands a level of awareness, a span of attention, and degree of concentration not to be expected from the general public. Modern music sometimes discourages even the specialists themselves. How can the mere amateur set about penetrating its mysteries? Certain problems of a very general nature do intrigue him and he likes to know where music is going, but that is enough.

The music of our own century interprets the preoccupations and the concerns of the world we live in. We must play it and listen to it, learn about advanced aesthetic positions, new theories of harmony, and new principles of construction, but this acquaintance is not made instantaneously.

It is certainly necessary to have heard a very large number of works of greater or lesser significance to be able to discover a masterpiece on the day of its birth. Posterity usually sorts them out for us.

Life goes so quickly these days that it takes a conscious effort to avoid being outdistanced. If we wish to function as active human beings rather than remain passive spectators, we must present to our audiences what we consider important.

There is only one proper attitude to take toward the music of our own time: be patient, open our hearts, listen without prejudice and without snobbery. André Gide has said, 'Always be on an incline but always be on the way up.'

Young musicians always want to create a movement at any cost and they always want to impose it on others. They try to do so with ardor and often with insolence, with the expectation of freeing themselves from a past they scorn and disdain, and without the smallest concern for the masters who also sought, struggled, and suffered.

Every creative force has its roots in the past but every composer finds his own language as he works. Listen to the young Strauss and hear Mendelssohn; Debussy, Massenet; Schoenberg, Wagner; Stravinsky, Rimsky-Korsakov.

Be that as it may, it is our duty to bring out the young composers and to encourage them, while seeking to discover as best we can their true value. A conductor must be a treasure hunter. This is a duty he too often neglects but one that may gain him the greatest recognition in his own time. I for one have had the good fortune to live among such musicians as Roussel, Honegger, Schmitt, Messiaen, Martinu, when they still needed to be played. In twenty years the list will be much longer for the history of music has no end. Tomorrow's conductors will not have to envy their elders. It will be for them to forge the glory of composers still unknown.

* * *

A few more problems:

You have fallen madly in love with a certain score. One day its charms seem to have exhausted themselves. Love flies out the window. How to react? The best thing, under these circumstances, is a separation until love is reborn, as it may well be one day.

There are also such things as neglected masterpieces. Take careful note that I do not believe in 'forgotten masterpieces,' although there are people who make a profession of rediscovering them, people who sift through the musical rubble of centuries past, from which time has already separated the valuables.

But I know works that are greatly respected though they fall just a little short of being true masterpieces. Sometimes a slight abridgment gives them a more favorable shape, just as cutting gives a diamond its full value. The composer may have neglected this essential operation himself. This is a problem to be faced, I think, in the magnificent symphony of Paul Dukas. If no cuts are made, if its present form is respected to the letter, it will disappear forever. I do not think it barbarous to say that everything possible must be done to save it from that undeserved fate.

Another example is the charming symphony Bizet wrote when he was seventeen years old. If you play it in its original form, it will seem just too long for its substance. If you make a few little cuts without throwing the form into a new state of unbalance and without sacrificing a single musical element, you sense its real beauties and you possess yet another jewel.

5

Face to Face with the Score

How EXCITING an orchestra score is. All those staffs one above the other—twenty or twenty-four or more—the paper speckled with notes and countless signs. This is what you must analyze and bring to life, love and make others love.

It is an indisputable fact that no other art has created so difficult an instrument, so complex a medium of expression as the symphony orchestra. The pages on which the orchestra's 'actions' are described are not easy reading. I cannot explain completely here the machinery of the orchestra score, but I shall try to give my lay readers an idea of what it is.

45

For one thing, it is a great invention, one of the most ingenious products of the human mind left unrecognized by intellectual historians, an achievement overlooked in the age of 'science.' The score can best be comprehended by the non-musician as a device for writing down twenty or forty or more simultaneous speeches, each one of which may be in a different language but every word with its proper accent, inflection, and nuance.

On each page are the lines played by every instrument, arranged in groups one above the other:

1. the woodwinds: flutes, oboes, clarinets, bassoons
2. the brasses: horns, trumpets, trombones, tubas
3. the percussion: timpani, snare drum, bass drum, cymbals, xylophone, castanets; even typewriter, airplane propeller, and whatnot
4. the strings: violins, violas, cellos, basses.

In addition to all this, the harps, the piano, and the organ are also separate categories. In the case of a concerto or an opera or an oratorio, there are lines for soloists and chorus too.

Every note played or sung by any or all of these forces appears on the score page, together with an indication of how it is to be played: loud or soft, attached to the next note or separated from it, with strong accents or with none at all. Horizontally you read the lines and see the voice-leading, the

46

counterpoint; vertically, the superimposition of many different kinds of sound and the harmony. The conductor must know how to see and hear all this. Reading a score and conducting it, he must always know where every single line is going and how they all sound together.

As if this is not already difficult enough, there is the further burden of the transposing instruments. Their notes in the conductor's score are not actually the notes that sound but a corresponding series on another level chosen to facilitate the task of the player—and several different wind instruments are on several different levels.

Middle C in the first and second horns may be almost any other two notes. Among the clarinets, what looks like middle C may be the E-flat or D above or may actually be the C (which is very unlikely) but is probably the B-flat below or perhaps the A. And I omit four other members of the clarinet family found in music from Mozart to Strauss.

There are scores without these transpositions, in which everything is written in the same key for the conductor's sake and every written note represents the actual sound produced. The facilitating transpositions appear only in the players' parts. Honegger and Prokofieff are among the most important modern composers who have used this rational system. But musicians' habits and the large stocks in the libraries and the publishers' warehouses will prevent wider dissemination of this usage, I fear. We shall continue to suffer for some time with this practice, for which history does in fact provide proper reasons that are no longer valid. For years to come our Berlioz scores will have the horn parts in four different keys.

These are just a few of the technical problems— and furnish good reason for getting down to work.

* * *

Now you are sitting at your desk. Your week's work, three or four folio-size scores, barely leave space for the accumulation of odds and ends, for the letters you have not had time to answer, the baton you dropped the evening before when you got back from the concert, the telephone which must at any price be prevented from ringing. The careful study of a score requires peace, silence, and time. Lock your door and open the score that begins your next concert to its first page.

When you go on stage for the first rehearsal, you must already know the score as well as you ever will. Music lovers learn their favorite works from repeated hearing. The conductor must know them a thousand times more thoroughly and he must learn them from the printed page.

Is your first score some standard work that you have already played a hundred times? Do you think you know it by heart? Are you sure? Even so, every time you prepare it for performance you

48

must also prepare yourself by restudying it just as though you had never seen it before. Is it a complicated contemporary work? Can you think of ways to ease its difficulties for your musicians? Will the facilitating device achieve precisely the same effect? Your study desk is the place to solve this problem.

The difficulties of analysis are considerable with contrapuntal writing, notably Bach's. He is truly the founder and the master of continuous development. He submits for examination a block of faultless marble. But do not be discouraged. Continue your searches. Musical construction has its likenesses to sentence structure. There are commas and semicolons, periods, question marks, and exclamation points. Sometimes there should be quotation marks too—but that is another story. Music stops and starts, breathes. You must find out where and when. An interpretation that does not take this essential fact into account is sure to be monotonous. It will be boring or altogether incomprehensible, like a literary text read aloud with no consideration of punctuation, of phrase or clause or sentence.

When you have finished this analysis look back over it and see how the musical net is woven. Evaluate the significance of every phrase. This will get you down to a harmonic analysis in which you will find what the primary and secondary elements are.

One single note among a hundred may determine the significance and the function of a chord.

All these are things that you must know about your score even before you have heard it.

* * *

I am often asked if I hear the music I read, if I am listening to an orchestra when I run my eyes over a page of score. I think that all conductors of any accomplishment find no difficulty whatsoever in hearing in their minds what they read in *classical* scores. They have seen and heard enough in the style to be able to fathom one they may never have seen before by a simple exercise of memory and association.

The exercise becomes more difficult with modern music, in which composers may seek strange effects, in which the orchestration is an element of considerable importance and mixes sounds that we do not often hear juxtaposed. It is simply a matter of auditory habituation, or of listening to new things in new ways. Our descendants, who will grow up with the sounds that are new to us, will think them normal and classical—or perhaps just old-fashioned and valueless.

* * *

To be sure of suffering no slips of the ear, the wisest thing to do is to take your scores to the piano and pick out the notes. This is an excellent exercise. It requires you to seek out the essentials and

50

to pursue the materials no matter where they may go.

There is no better way to be absolutely sure of gaining insight into a score's every secret than to learn it by heart. Memorizing requires the highest degree of concentration and attention to the most minute musical detail. Begin by reading and retaining phrase by phrase the sound of the separate parts and then of the family groups. Then put them all together in your mind, imagining a sonorous synthesis of all the instruments. This is of the greatest importance, for in rehearsal you must be able to indicate to an oboe or a trombone or the solo violin the exact instant when he is to separate himself from the orchestral mass and present an idea with the voice and weight that are his own.

* * *

It goes without saying that when you are performing a new work for the first time you must be particularly careful. In the case of a composition already played but new to you, you may be lucky enough to get hold of a recording, which will be very helpful in studying and preparing your own interpretation and performance.

If you are the first to decipher and shed light on a difficult modern work, do not be discouraged easily. Read the score sympathetically and be surprised at nothing. You can soon tell whether the composer is to be taken seriously or not. In the

51

latter case, the best course of action is to close the score and to throw it on the heap under the piano. In the former, look up the composer's telephone number and invite him to come see you. The best way of solving the maze of a complex contemporary work is with the guidance of the Daedalus who created the labyrinth.

Put the score on the piano and ask him to show you exactly how he wants it to go. Keep calm and clear-headed without stilling your capacity for enthusiasm. Do as much of your preparatory work as possible with the help of the composer, but do not forget that he may have put many things into his score of whose existence he is hardly aware. It is the interpreter's privilege to discover them.

Debussy, listening to his String Quartet being tried out for the first time, said to the musicians, 'You play the third movement twice as fast as I thought it should go.' Then he paused a moment to enjoy the disturbance he had created and added, 'But it's so much better your way!'

* * *

This brings up a question of the rights of the performer. For three hundred years the orchestra has been changing. When Beethoven used the horns in his symphonies, he did so with discretion and often with regret, we think now, that he could not give them an even greater role to play. In his time the horns had certain mechanical limitations

52

that no longer exist. You can sense these limitations when you come upon holes in the orchestration, places where Beethoven had to take the horns out—even in the middle of a phrase. The gaps are easy to fill. The benefits derived from this small license are obvious, but Beethoven did not leave us word that should a day come when the horns could freely play chromatically he would be happy to have them do so in his works. When I take it upon myself to make modifications of this kind, I feel that I do not betray Beethoven but remain faithful to his spirit. It is a burden on my conscience nevertheless.

It is curious that this problem never arises in the music of Haydn and Mozart, perhaps because they, in the generation before Beethoven, were content with the instruments as they found them and did not seek to exceed the resources available to them.

Points like this must be examined at home. When you are with the orchestra, it will be too late to start thinking about them.

* * *

Many conductors are so conscientious and exacting in their preparatory work that they write precise instructions into each musician's part. This is not a useless precaution but when ten conductors of this kind have had turns with the same orchestra, the music is covered with a mass of contradictory hieroglyphics. Every such conductor should have his own library of parts. Furthermore, this kind of work requires many hours of tedious labor and for conductors as for everyone else, modern life is not very generous with hours. I am satisfied with seeing that uniform bowings are written into the string parts—that all the bows go up and down together for the sake of good string tone—which may save some time later. The winds are individualists who learn quickly in rehearsal.

* * *

You have a perfect right to a conception of music based on your own temperament. You may imagine a musical work to have subject matter or you may wish to avoid translating it into pictures or ideas, but performance must be a means of expression at least as eloquent and as direct as any visual impression.

Music always suggests something to me: just a color or a landscape or perhaps a sensation that can be felt and expressed only in sound. My taste for painting often brings visual images to mind to mix with sounds.

The problem of the image is relatively simple with a work like Beethoven's *Pastoral Symphony*, for the composer took care to leave us explanatory notes that we can only follow without debate.

And consider Berlioz. With all his clumsiness and his bad basses, he succeeds in making the tempestuously romantic impression he strove for. In France we do not set 'I love you' in invertible counterpoint. Berlioz owes his genius to his spontaneity. He became the Delacroix of music not by building according to rigid specifications but by working in big frescoes spattered with broad splashes of color. Everything is more than life-size. It would be frustrating to try to listen to this music the way one looks at an exquisite miniature.

In the end, almost all music is descriptive for me but sometimes I experience visual impressions that the composer had no intention of arousing. Debussy's *La Mer* is identified with the Mediterranean. In fact it might just as well be the Atlantic or the Channel (though never the Dead Sea), but in the third movement I always return to *terra firma* in spite of myself and see autumn leaves falling gently to earth. The music of Strauss is very 'visual' for me, Ravel's less so than you might expect.

It should always be possible to make out the composer's image in the music. The conductor must discover and show what the creator wanted understood.

Perhaps you think the public lacking in imagination and that everything must be made obvious for it? At one point in the score of *Romeo and Juliet* Berlioz inserted this note:

'The public has no imagination. Therefore works that are addressed to the imagination have no public. The following scene being of this sort, I think it must be omitted when this symphony is performed for any but an elite audience, that is ninety-nine times out of a hundred.'

I think Berlioz was a little pessimistic but it is none the less true that the public will not strain itself to hang a dream on every note. It is for us to facilitate their task.

* * *

When you close your last score of the week, you should have all the music on the program fixed in your mind. You should have foreseen the places where you must give special attention to the musicians you have found to have the most serious problems. You should have discovered the place where a mistake in the strings or perhaps the woodwinds seems inevitable. Above all you should know what to do to avoid these dangers.

For you, the game is played. There is nothing left but to communicate the results of your labors to the orchestra.

6

Rehearsing

WHEN YOU ARRIVE at the hall for your morning
rehearsal at five minutes to ten, do not open the
door marked 'Stage Entrance' right away. Stop for
a moment and listen to the formless and undis-
ciplined sounds emerging from the musicians'
room. The violinists are tuning up, playing scales
or passages from concertos. The winds are all exer-
cising hard too, bringing up the temperature of
their instruments in order to be in tune. They are
like athletes scattered around a stadium, stretching
and warming up before the game.

This atmosphere of musical anarchy is as exciting to a conductor as the smell of fresh printer's

57

ink to a journalist or the bouquet of a rare wine to a *Chevalier du Tastevin*. Little by little calm returns. The concert master performs his first task, to tune the instruments to the A he has taken from the first oboe. It is a custom of the greatest importance, observed throughout the world.

The orchestra must be made to give the impression of playing in tune although absolute accuracy in this is beyond the realm of possibility. One orchestra may play more or less nearly in tune than another—which makes an enormous difference. Aside from the mechanical limitations of the instruments and the human limitations of the players, notes actually become different when they belong to different keys. On the piano G-sharp and A-flat are the same, but for the orchestra G-sharp in the key of E major and A-flat in the key of F minor are two very different things. A better approximation of just intonation can often be obtained if you explain to the orchestra what is happening harmonically.

* * *

There you are in your place on stage. Before you sit a hundred men who hold in their hands instruments created for the purpose of making sounds of various kinds.

The orchestra is not a docile or mechanical instrument. It is a social body, a collection of human beings. It has a psychology and reflexes. It can be

58

guided but it must not be offended. First you must silence them.

I remember the conductor of an amateur orchestra in Strasbourg who hung a big bell from his stand. Before beginning to rehearse he used to ring it furiously to let his presence be known. Happily, those days are gone, together with the cudgel blows of the baton nervously beating the measure on the back of the stand.

This was a vestige of the means employed by conductors of long ago, the remains of the method invented in the seventeenth century by Lulli—the first true conductor in the modern sense—who used a big heavy stick and introduced the authoritarian mannerisms so dear to many of his successors. Didn't he once break his violin over the head of a recalcitrant musician? Recalcitrant musicians are still to be found but one no longer breaks violins over their heads. This over-energetic measure helps neither performance nor discipline.

* * *

How is the orchestra arranged on the stage?

First of all, the acoustical qualities of the hall must be taken into account. This is a precaution that is often neglected but is nevertheless very important. I remember a concert at the Paris Opera at which I died a thousand deaths because despite the imposing array of forces we used, all the music rose to the stage flies. The entire mass of three hundred choral singers standing behind the orchestra seemed to have been struck dumb.

I usually arrange the strings with first and second violins together at my left, cellos upstage and violas downstage at my right. In this way the violas, whose importance is often undervalued, are brought out more and are heard better.

The loud voices of the orchestra, the trumpets and trombones, may be relegated to a place on the side. I put them on a slant so that their bells will not point directly into the hall. The woodwinds are in two rows in the center of the stage, with the four first-players as close together as possible. The horns curve behind them. The percussion is at the back on the left and the basses on the right, good neighbors of the cellos.

This topography is the one that seems to me to give the best results, the greatest coherence and the finest balance.

* * *

The sole purpose of the rehearsal is work—and what a mistake to believe that it is only for the orchestra and not for the conductor. No soloist would dream of appearing in public without practicing on his instrument and the orchestra is the conductor's instrument. I have heard some illustrious conductors claim that they never make mistakes. When something goes wrong it is never their fault, lucky fellows. I take the opposite position.

If a horn player or some other wind player misses a note because his lips are tired, the conductor obviously can do nothing about it. But an accident of that kind is unimportant. It is quite improper to fly into a rage on account of such a peccadillo and to look daggers at the guilty man, already sorry enough himself for his squawk. But of course it is a matter of principle that a conductor can let nothing go by, no faulty entry, no wrong note. He must stop and play the questionable passage over again as many times as he finds necessary—even though musicians generally do not like to.

* * *

What attitude should the conductor take toward the musicians to obtain the best results?

Let him not make long speeches to them. Musicians come to play, not to listen to lectures. Say what you must in as few words as possible. Experienced professionals hate to be given lessons. Let them retain some sense of responsibility. Never discourage them. Restore the confidence of those who are in trouble. Do not make much of their errors. Correct them without embarrassing them before their comrades.

Do you distrust the musicians' judgment? They are quick to discover the true quality of their conductor. Richard Strauss's father, a famous horn player, once came right out and said, 'Remember

61

this, you conductors. We watch you step up on the podium and open your score. Before you pick up your baton, we know if it is you or we who will be master.' In the same vein, there is the story of a cynical musician who, when asked what a famous guest conductor's program was to be, answered, 'I don't know what he's going to conduct but we are playing Beethoven's Fifth.'

There is no question about it. Musicians know right away if you have the authority to be their leader, if you are 'somebody.' Authority emanates from a strong personality. In his wonderful book, *The Art of Conducting,* Wagner wrote, 'Only orchestra musicians have the capacity to judge good and bad conducting.' He made no mistake.

* * *

With new works the first rehearsal is devoted to a plain reading, to discover the inevitable mistakes in the music and to acquaint the musicians with the technical difficulties that face them. It is like showing the obstacles to the thoroughbred before the race.

There are many passages in the orchestral literature that are easy to conduct but hard to play. With a particularly problematic work it is often profitable to have sectional rehearsals first, the winds at one time and the strings another. Give the musicians a chance to figure out what the notes are and do not bother with expression. At the next

62

rehearsal of the whole orchestra everything will have been deciphered and all the parts will fall into their proper places. Classical works obviously do not need this kind of preparation.

* * *

What is there to say about tempos?

Gluck said, 'Just a bit too fast or a bit too slow and all is lost.' A *presto* is obvioulsy not an *andante* nor an *adagio* an *allegro*. All music has its own inner pace that belongs to it as branches belong to a tree. To want to change it for another or even to modify it would be criminal. I often think of the reply of a great master, if I may tell another story, who when asked about a proper tempo for a certain classical work, said, 'If you don't know what tempo to take, don't take any!'

You do not feel music the same way every day. Fritz Kreisler used to tell a story about a performance of the Brahms concerto under the composer's direction. Once, late in life, Brahms attacked the finale at a dizzying speed, much faster than usual. Kreisler stopped and protested but Brahms said, 'Why not, my dear friend? My pulse is faster than usual today.' What a wonderful excuse. It is too bad that only musicians as great as Brahms can use it. The rest of us must plan as much as possible before going on stage—even the pulse rate.

A critic once reproached Richard Strauss, who was an incomparable conductor, for having conducted the finale of a Mozart symphony too fast. Strauss said, 'These gentlemen of the press seem to have a direct wire to Olympus.'

Is there a simple rule by which the one true tempo may be discovered? I do not think so but Kreisler has laid down this general principle: 'Where the notes are few and large in value, don't slow down the beat. Where there are many short notes, take your time.' If you follow this, you will at least approach the truth.

There are obviously many problems here. We are not machines, happily. We can make mistakes. It happens to everyone. But if you interpret music as you feel it, with ardor and faith, with all your heart and with complete conviction, I am certain that even if the critics attack you, God will forgive you.

* * *

The proper dynamic nuances are easy to obtain if you indicate them clearly and precisely with your stick. *Piano* and *diminuendo* are always somewhat more difficult to obtain than *forte* and *crescendo*.

The essentials to get from the musicians are respect for the exact value of each note, 'singing' tone, and elimination of all elements that are out of the style of the piece—and without theorizing. Musicians are generally not intellectuals. Address yourself to their feelings to get them into the spirit of a piece. They will understand immediately.

The problem of balancing sounds of different weights deserves special attention. Every element must be properly placed in musical relief. The principal voices must be brought forward without suppressing the rest. You must be able to prevent the brasses from covering the strings and make any single instrument emerge from a tutti. The sounds play about you like waves and you must put each one in its proper place. This is difficult for you because what you hear on the stage often gives a poor impression of how the music sounds in the hall. You must sometimes descend from your pedestal and take a seat in the last row to listen, just as you look at a picture from a distance.

* * *

It goes without saying that all this takes time and that not all orchestras work at the same pace. With the best of them it is a good idea not to over-rehearse. You must have confidence in the musicians' receptivity and spontaneity.

A mediocre orchestra requires more attention and care but I for one have never disdained any orchestra. I find it interesting to work with some of the less finished groups. Their good will and enthusiasm often more than compensate for their lack of technical attainment. I have many happy memories of conducting orchestras of young musicians and provincial semi-professional orchestras.

* * *

I still want to take up here three special situations where experience is helpful.

The first: Playing a new work. If it can be arranged, the composer's presence at rehearsals is of the greatest value. If he has a thorough knowledge of conducting, perhaps the composer himself can best realize the intentions of the work.

The second: Accompanying a soloist. A feeling of friendly co-operation between conductor and soloist is of the greatest importance, but such a feeling is not always easy to achieve. There are times when everything can be arranged amicably, but in case of incompatibility do you follow a soloist who is going against your wishes? I think the conductor cannot do otherwise. If he tries to slow down or hurry up a soloist he risks a catastrophe.

When Goethe was director of the theater at Weimar he once had to arbitrate a dispute between one of his opera singers and an excellent conductor. He ruled in favor of the singer and the conductor was dismissed. It would be better if the directors, even when they are men like Goethe, would not interfere.

When you are accompanying, it is not enough that you hear the soloist's every note or that you understand the singer's every word. Can the audience hear and understand? The singer's diction is your responsibility. The public has a right to understand the words. You cannot expect it to know by heart all the lines in a scene from a Wagner opera.

The third: Recording. This is becoming a separate profession. It supposes close co-operation between the conductor and the technicians, who are not necessarily musicians. At recording sessions you will find yourself repeating passages over and over again and very profitably, for the playing back of what has just been recorded lets you hear exactly what you have done and shows you what you can improve.

* * *

In music more than anywhere else, our deeds pursue us. We should never forget that it is for us to please those who listen.

7

Concerts

THERE REALLY SHOULD NOT BE very much to say about the concert, since the conductor's role there is to be noticed as little as possible.

Nevertheless a concert day is not like all the other days. It is a celebration, but with too many preliminaries. There is the self-styled intimate friend who grabs your coattail and asks for a seat. There is the problem of replacing the horn or trombone player fallen ill since the final rehearsal. There is the occasional soloist who hides in a corner of the artists' room paralyzed with fear, whimpering, 'I can't go on.' And then there is the bother of dressing, which some artists are superstitious

about. And speaking of superstition, there are conductors who do not dare go on stage if they have
not figured out in advance how to get to their
stands in exactly thirteen steps.

I am happy not to have come to that. These are
all things that should be erased from your con-
sciousness when you set out on the sinuous path
through the orchestra to the center of the stage.

The lights go down. Conversation in the hall,
murmurs in the orchestra are stilled. This is the
profound and beautiful silence that precedes the
first note of music.

* * *

What is to be expected of the conductor during
the concert? In principle he has a very simple role
to play. He has carefully prepared everything in
the most minute detail. He has done his work and
is only a figurehead now. But it is not a useless
tradition that keeps the chief at the head of his
troops during the battle.

In our day, an orchestra without a conductor is
inconceivable. Our orchestras often consist of more
than a hundred men whose actions must be integrated and co-ordinated—especially as new music
becomes more and more complex.

And then the conductor must be there to inspire
the musicians and to instill in them the emotions
the music arouses in him. He has two ways of com-
municating with them, facial expression and ges-

ture. The look in his eyes is often more important than the motion of a baton or the position of a hand. He may even use pantomime, but cautiously, for the conductor must be neither clown nor gymnast. Happy, gay, amusing music must never be conducted with a funereal mien, although I have often seen it done.

The left and right hands have missions that are complementary but quite different. The right delineates the meter. It must be light and clear but the motions it makes as it designs the beat in the air obey carefully drawn rules that may be broken only at the risk of throwing the orchestra into confusion. It is of the greatest importance that the gestures be prevented from contradicting the desired expression. What shall the musicians do if your gestures require *forte* while you do not hide your displeasure at their not playing *piano?*

The precision of the first attack is of enormous importance. If it is shaky, it is no good. It must be clear and indicate in space the exact duration of the beat, the basic matter in the tempo you are going to take.

The degree of independence of a conductor's arms is a good indication of the importance he attaches to sensitivity of interpretation. The left hand entreats the orchestra and points out which phrase should be more thrilling, which more calm, more spacious, more gentle, more tender.

Every conductor acquires a vocabulary of gestures that work for him, that explain what is going on inside. But he should never tie himself down to a system. It is versatility that counts and there must be as many gradations of motion as there are of sound.

The right hand draws, the left hand colors. If you think and truly feel the music within you with all the concentration and will at your command, everything falls into place. Let the music be fixed in your mind so firmly that it seems to spring like Minerva from the head of Zeus, full-grown.

* * *

The spark, the electric current that must emanate from the conductor, is what makes a performance that was carefully prepared in rehearsal become at concert time a masterful one or, as the critics—who do not always have good memories—say, an unforgettable one.

An important factor in your success is in the public's hands. Audience receptivity is variable. Sometimes when I think everything is going well, I do not arouse the reaction I expect. Perhaps I expect too much, but a responsive audience creates an environment favorable to good performances.

* * *

It has been said, 'You must play what is written.' But it has also been said, 'The most important things are between the notes.'

71

Both statements are correct and they are not contradictory. It is impossible to play 'between the
notes' without playing what is written.

It has been said that music is the art of expressing opinions through depth of feeling. The concert
is not the place to form new opinions. Concert
time is when feelings must be made to reach an
extreme of intensity. This is a fundamental mission of the conductor. Otherwise he is nothing but
a traffic policeman directing the movement of
many lanes of music through a complicated inter-
section—or an officer charged with making certain
that orders previously given are meticulously observed.

* * *

Verdi used to protest strongly against the tyr-
anny of conductors who made music pass between
the Caudine Forks of their personal aesthetic, dis-
regarding completely the wishes of the composer.
We often hear said these days, speaking of the Fifth
Symphony by Beethoven, 'Have you heard X's
Fifth Symphony?' or 'Y's Fifth Symphony?' X and
Y being conductors famous for the whimsy of their
interpretations. I find this very distressing. I am interested in Beethoven's Fifth.

When you give the *première* of a new work, you
are a little like a knight doing battle for an ideal
which the public may not hold so high as you do.

72

But if you have faith, and if you hold it and show it, you will help the novice reach his goal.

Here you have a serious responsibility. If you are guilty of mutilating a piece that no one knows, how can anyone get an idea of its true quality? Even the poor composer won't know what to think about it.

How many examples there are of serious consequences to a disfiguring *première*. In the chapter on conducting he appended to his book on orchestration, Berlioz wrote,

'Singers have often been accused of being the most dangerous intermediary between composer and public but unjustly, I think. It is the conductor I fear the most. A bad singer can usually do harm only to his own part. An incompetent or ill-natured conductor can ruin everything. The composer whose work has fallen into the hands of conductors who are not incompetent or ill-natured or both may count himself fortunate, for nothing can resist their pernicious influence. The most marvelous orchestra can be paralysed, the best singers stilled and benumbed. There is no ensemble, no spirit. Under weak direction the composer's noblest and boldest outbursts seem extravagances. Enthusiasm is cut short. Inspiration is violently brought to earth. The angel is stripped of its wings. The man of genius becomes a fool and a blockhead. Idols are knocked from their pedestals and dragged through the mud.—And what is worse, with a new work being heard for the first time, it is impossible for the public, even for an audience of the highest musical intelligence, to know the conductor is playing havoc with the music, to discover his stupidity, his mistakes and the crimes that he is committing.'

* * *

Accompanying a soloist requires a calm head and cool blood at all times, a considerable exercise of technical skill, and a constant presence of mind. Sometimes a soloist gets lost or skips a few measures. Then without seeming to notice and especially without letting the public notice, the conductor must bring orchestra and soloist back together again. I remember one conductor who on such an occasion roared at the violins, 'Tremolo on C.' Then during the moment's respite from confusion, while they held the C, he let them know a good place where they could all meet and continue.

Sometimes one accompanies singers who seem to have laid bets on not keeping up with everyone else. Saint-Saëns used to tell a funny story about a time when he was trying to accompany two young girls in a duet. They were never together. Finally he stopped, looked at them seriously, and said, 'Now tell me, which one of you two am I supposed to accompany?'

* * *

Let us never forget that we are music's servants. How may one dare to speak of more or less spectacular conductors? The conductor isn't there to put on a show for the audience. A conductor worthy of the name is too busy making his feelings known to the orchestra to remember which is his better profile or to guess what flattering pose may have the best effect on the people sitting behind him. He must always know exactly what he is doing *about his music* so that the musicians may know exactly what they are to do.

Conducting a concert involves a prodigious expenditure of nervous energy. Berlioz tells in his *Memoirs* that after a performance of his overture *Francs-Juges* he stretched out across the timpani exhausted and sobbed. I do not see anything to laugh about in this story. He had conducted a work of his own, had consumed a little of his soul. Every musical interpreter must be capable of this kind of complete confession. If he is not, he will have to change his trade.

* * *

It is often said that some conductor is excellent in the theater but poor in concert or vice versa. I do not understand this position at all. It seems to me that it is neither more nor less difficult to make a soprano sing in time than a solo violin. Making an orchestra play *piano* requires equal subtlety whether accompanying a coloratura or the flute in

Debussy's *Faune*. In either case it is a matter of attaining maximum expressivity—within the limitations of the performers.

The true conductor will never be sparing of his talent or of effort even if he is playing before an audience of three people in a terrible hall while suffering an attack of jaundice. Under the best of conditions or the worst, if he has a bad day all his sins will be forgiven if he only proves his emotion and his fervor.

These days mechanics and athletics have taken over everything and 'objectivity' is demanded of us. We should be ashamed of our feelings, ashamed of being sensitive or even sentimental, in the best sense of the word. We are still allowed to listen with our ears but not with our hearts. We may no longer even sing with spirit.

If artists can no longer be sensitive, why not require that scholars behave like idiots. Was Beethoven wrong when he wrote on the manuscript of his *Missa Solemnis,* 'This comes from the heart. May it touch the heart.' I refuse to think so.

8

The Musician's Life

THE MOST SOLEMN MOMENT in the preparation of a concert is the one when you establish your first contact with an orchestra that you are not acquainted with or that you have not conducted for a long time. It is not an orchestra that you are facing then but a hundred human beings, each one of whom knows joy and pain and suffering. Before telling them, as I usually do, how pleased I am to be able to make music with them, I always look at those hundred faces turned up to me. I try to read what is in their eyes, to discover the happiness or sometimes, alas, the misery hidden there. I try to find what role each one plays in the *comédie hu-*

maine. This is a short and silent communion, reaching into the bottom of the heart, engendering a climate of sympathy, friendliness, and trust. People who hate one another should not be allowed to make music together.

I want to speak here of the lot of the modest and anonymous orchestra musicians who are sometimes more talented than the famous soloists they accompany. It is proper to pay them homage, for what would a conductor be without them? After all, it is they who play—not the conductor and not the manager.

* * *

In most parts of the world the musical profession is badly organized. Musicians must trust to luck or to their skill in business. Talent is not always the first consideration of organizers of orchestras. They are more often concerned with budgets than art. When they have recruited a few good first-desk players, they consider their work well done and are then satisfied with just filling up the rest of the chairs on the stage. Their methods resemble those of the buccaneers of old who filled out the complement of their crews without being too particular about seamanship.

* * *

How to become an orchestra musician?

Conservatory students are endowed with great ambition. They dream of world-wide fame and the

78

careers they will make as soloists. You must have known these dreams yourself to understand the orchestra musician's psychology, to measure the disenchantment of a prize pupil who finds himself one fine day in possession of a handsome diploma but with no opportunity to be heard. Recital giving is expensive and the impresarios do not line up to come running with contracts when you ring.

Happily, musicians do not always join orchestras out of disillusion, though often out of necessity. The taste for it comes later. At least I hope it does.

Most conservatories have now been induced to supplement their instruction by forming student orchestras in which their pupils may acquire at least the spirit that is indispensable in a properly integrated orchestra. Though they may still dream of independent careers, the young musicians learn among their comrades to love music as it should be loved—unselfishly. They learn that there is a loftiness in the profession of the orchestral musician and treasure its memory even if they abandon it.

*   *   *

The daily existence of an orchestral musician presents difficulties that only the love of music makes endurable.

In some cases, playing violin or clarinet in one of the regular Paris Sunday concert series is almost a philanthropic act. I am thinking of specific cases.

The musicians band together to give one or sometimes two concerts a week. At the end of the year
they share the profits. When the members of one
of the best orchestras in Paris divided their infini-
tesimal profits among themselves after a recent full
season of rehearsals and concerts, each one had
earned the equivalent of $1.45 per service. They
had played three rehearsals and at least one concert
every week of the season for about $6.00 per week.
The disproportion between time spent in carefully
preparing the pleasures of Parisian music lovers
and the gain received is painfully evident and sadly
eloquent.

Such orchestras continue to exist because they
are business centers and hiring halls. During rehearsal intermissions, the fifteen minutes reserved
to the cigarette, the musicians often find their
other engagements that are financially more re-
warding.

Among orchestral musicians there are the more
privileged who belong to the national opera and
radio orchestras. They are fortunate in that they
receive regular salaries and are allowed to combine
their official positions with occasional engagements. They make records, play for films, in
churches, in the homes of the wealthy.

But all this adds up to a working day of eighteen
hours almost without interruption. Such a musician's daily schedule accounts for every minute in

the day. And music is counted among the 'liberal' professions!

The lure of a big income is not the motivating force behind this feverish activity. The mere necessities of life, food, lodging, and clothes, are as important to musicians as to everyone else. In the vast majority of cases musicians cannot afford a moment's respite if they are to make ends meet.

Always working or on the run, that is the musician's lot. Never to be sure of the next day, never to have the security of a regular salary that can calm the shooting pains of anxiety in the struggle for his daily bread—is there any other priesthood that demands so much of its priests?

And then when can he find time to practice by himself? Playing in an orchestra, playing no matter how many concerts does not replace the valuable hours of work that a musician should have in the solitude of his studio—hours essential to staying on top. And when shall he find the no less necessary time for relaxing his nerves and refreshing his spirits?

Consideration is not often enough given to their physical labors. They work like galley slaves but like slaves intoxicated by the fresh sea air.

In addition, it is not generally understood how hard the work itself is. The public cannot imagine what exhausting toil it is for the brasses, for example, to play a Wagner opera. For the rest of the orchestra, even for the strings, it is killing to play five hours at a stretch.

To earn as many fees as possible becomes an obsession. I think it miraculous that under the circumstances musicians still keep their enthusiasm, their faith in music, and their love of their profession.

A few years ago I toured the entire United States with the *Orchestre National de la Radiodiffusion Française,* the French National Radio Orchestra. We had great successes wherever we went. It is a wonderful orchestra and is still talked about. But it is not generally known under what conditions we made that trip. First, we traveled by bus. Then after 300 miles on the road, always too hot or too cold and always dirty, we arrived somewhere or other, tired out and usually behind schedule. The musicians, men and women too (and the women's courage throughout the trip was altogether admirable), often had to play without even a chance to change from their traveling clothes or to restore their spirits with a cup of coffee. Those of us who made that tour will never forget the kindness of the good people of Montreal who, hearing of our miseries and knowing that we had arrived hungry and thirsty, immediately ordered fifty roast chickens for an after-concert supper. The concert was a good one, the chickens delicious.

* * *

In all the conservatories of both the old world and the new, little notices appear on the bulletin boards at the end of every school year announcing auditions in one orchestra or another for a viola player or a second bassoon or bass drum. But it is heartbreaking to admit that all the orchestras in the world—in Paris they can be counted on the fingers of one hand and in New York there is practically only one—cannot provide places for all the qualified musicians turned out by the schools and conservatories every year.

Remarkable talents go to waste. Some take refuge in small towns where they establish themselves as teachers. Others form the nuclei of impoverished provincial orchestras whose membership consists chiefly of amateurs. Smaller cities in the United States recruit musicians for their part-time orchestras by offering them employment in factories and stores. In France how many simply beat the pavements of Paris looking for work. On a fine spring day there not long ago I saw a crowd of unemployed musicians on the street where a documentary film was being made, hoping to be engaged to play in a little street band.

Many musicians not at first so inclined end up playing jazz—and they are not the farthest from their goal. Too many are obliged to abandon the art they love. I was once driven to a concert at the Salle Pleyel in Paris by a taxi driver who told me that he was a first-prize winner at the Conservatory. And it is to France that all the world comes looking for musicians who will maintain the quality of the greatest orchestras.

I have conducted all over the world. I have found French musicians everywhere, especially French oboists, who are as much in demand as the greatest wines of Burgundy and Bordeaux. The world is not enough aware of the great human richness that France exports.

And everywhere I have admired the spirit and the high ideals of the great orchestras. Each has its own character, its own color, and its own special quality. But the musicians always know that they are only individual cells of a larger body. They know that they are completely dependent on one another and they place all their talent at the service of the musical collective of which each is but a part. They teach us an important lesson in human solidarity. It is an honor to conduct them.

Sometimes the head of an orchestra section comes forward from the ranks to play a concerto. His comrades never fail to give him the best support and to applaud him without any reservation or any suspicion of jealousy. But a true orchestra musician does not dream of making solo playing his career. Outside of the orchestra, he is probably more inclined to chamber music and may well spend his rare free evenings playing quartets or

84

trios with his colleagues. I know many world-famous ensembles of this kind that are made up of musicians who are still also members of orchestras and who consider the foundation of their musical lives to be still within this great family, which they will never abandon.

* * *

Next time you go to a concert, look at the orchestra on stage before the conductor's entrance. You probably cannot connect any of the names in the program book with the faces you see, but they deserve your respect and admiration just the same —and just as much as the famous virtuosi who prefer their glorious isolation to the splendid anonymity of the orchestra.

The Conductor's Life

THE FIRST TIME I saw my name printed on a program I had no suspicion of what fate held in store for me. Otherwise I should certainly not have chosen the eighth violin concerto of Ludwig Spohr for this point of departure in my career. I think I have never played it since. The poor concerto does not deserve such ingratitude, for this concert was the beginning of all my joy and all my sorrows. It was this that launched me on the monstrous and marvelous machine that the artist's life is.

I have always been interested in reading the lives of conductors of the past. Their lot seems hardly enviable at first. Look at Haydn, a mere domestic in the palace of the Esterhazys, engaged for the purpose of arousing pleasure in his Prince with the aid of a heterogeneous assemblage of twelve other part-time servant-musicians for an orchestra. Look at von Bülow, tormented and badly treated by Wagner and Brahms in turn and by many others whom he upheld with all his soul and with no expectation of gratitude.

Yes, but how happy Haydn was to have fostered the flowering of Mozart's genius. How proud von Bülow of having revealed Brahms and Wagner to the world. All this makes the struggle worth while, makes all the petty disputes and the wrongs bearable.

* * *

What do we really know about the conductors of the past? Nothing or very little. Many had their hours of glory but history has preserved only a few of their names. A small number of critically very fuzzy appreciations have come down to us and that is all.

It would be priceless to know how Umlauf, after studying the score with Beethoven, conducted the Ninth Symphony; what Hans Richter did at Bayreuth to earn such praise from Wagner; how Habeneck charmed all Paris with the romantic symphonies. Then at least we might know what traditions to respect—for no week ever goes by in which a conductor is not attacked for breaking with tradition.

'What traditions?' I often ask myself. Until the eighteenth century there are only the slightest hints of tempos or dynamics in the manuscript and printed scores. In Bach's time we begin to find a few more suggestions. We can more often tell whether the music is to be generally loud or soft, fast or slow, but never more than that. Albert Schweitzer once said in jest, 'Only one thing is sure. No interpreter ever agrees with anyone else's interpretation.'

How to guess the tempos and the dynamics a composer really wanted? How to know exactly where truth lies hidden? How has every generation since the work's creation interpreted it for itself? And what has been the influence of the work upon the interpreters through the years? These are important questions but they are not for us to answer. Let the musicologists and the philosophers answer them. To bring the work to life, to give expression to the bare written notes, that is our historic mission and our good tradition.

Thanks to the phonograph record, the wishes of twentieth-century composers and the ideas of the conductors who played their works will not disappear into the oubliettes of history.

* * *

A conductor's day must be as rigorously regulated as strict counterpoint. He inflicts an iron discipline on himself in order to bear the burdens of his life and to keep his effectiveness. My method, my daily schedule, is not necessarily the best but it works for me, helps get the best return from my intense labors, and allows me to glean an occasional hour of leisure.

In the morning my mind is still fresh and everything seems to come easily and quickly. This is the best time to rehearse. Afternoons must be kept free. This is the time for receiving young composers looking for sponsors, soloists come for advice, and the time for reading new scores and making programs. For careful study of scores I am performing I prefer the silence of the night, when I get my second wind and the music engraves itself more quickly on my memory. The senses are sharpened by the day's excitement and, most important, I know that nothing will disturb the solitude, peace, and silence which are so rare and precious these days.

This regimen is obviously not very restful. You must never be ill or even indisposed. Imagine a conductor at work for three hours in a row with a stomach-ache or a cold in the head. He loses a large part of his powers, muddles through his job as quickly as possible to seek the comfort of an old

89

leather chair and some aspirin or bicarbonate of soda.

A conductor, like almost everyone in music and the theater, will of course not eat much before a performance. He will take only light nourishment and not burden his body with the process of digestion when he needs all his strength for his work.

* * *

A conductor with a regular post giving him full responsibility for an orchestra is in a more difficult position—and a more interesting one—than the guest conductor. He is responsible to the public for every artistic aspect of his orchestra's entire season. He makes dozens of different programs, finds new works to bring out, chooses choral works or soloists and their concertos for variety. He has the advantage of knowing that he will be in the same place for more than a week or two at a time, sleep in the same bed, rehearse the same musicians in the same hall. He knows what to expect at concert time from both the orchestra and the public. But he must sustain their interest and keep fresh their appetite for music during week after week through a long season.

The guest conductor, on the other hand, is a kind of shooting star. He makes his sudden appearance, blazes brilliantly for the moment, and passes on hoping to have left a good impression behind. All traveling performers know the innu-

90

merable misadventures that can befall them on tour. You miss a train, a plane is late, a ship delayed by a storm, and a concert is crossed from your calendar. Or you arrive in a strange city to stand the next morning in front of an orchestra of unknown character and quality, to find yourself suddenly in a completely strange climate in which, without time to accustom yourself to it, you must work at your best. You are condemned to an eternal battle and you must always win.

And what about your public? People love music everywhere but do not show their enthusiasm in the same ways all over the world. Be happy when they whistle at you in Chicago but not in London. In one city, when the audience is perfectly silent at the end of your concert, you may play an encore. In another the applause may make you think you have achieved some kind of wild triumph yet not mean a thing. If you are saddened at being received with only reserved enthusiasm in Amsterdam, perhaps no conductor before you has ever had such a success with the warm-hearted but severely critical Dutch public.

In moving from place to place, take care not to be elated by failure or discouraged by success! To resist this constantly changing wind, this blowing of hot and cold that you must bear in addition to all your work, you must have a strong mind, a solid philosophy, and nerves of steel. How far ours is

91

from those occupations where the office door can be closed on all cares at five o'clock. This constant tension would be absolutely unbearable without a little leisure, an occasional distraction.

Most of the time you finish by renouncing almost everything not directly connected with conducting. You are submerged by the urgencies of your calling, for they allow no delay. But it is a mistake to submit to them completely.

The interpreter's career is different from the creator's but surely it is just as exacting. You must always have an open mind and a heart accessible to new ideas of beauty. Now I do not believe that any human being can forever consume his spirit or scatter his energies without wishing to receive something that will restore his strength and help him maintain a regenerating contact with the rest of the world. A plant plucked from the earth may produce one last flower but it will soon fade, wither, and die. Only a live bird sings.

Every artist knows at what fountain he finds comfort and strength. When I want a free and peaceful hour, I slip away to the antique shops, the old print dealers, and the second-hand book stores. Even if I don't buy anything, I am happy when I can just look around and dream. These hours of relaxation are alas too few. I have been in too many cities where I have not even had time to visit the museum.

Then there is reading. I sleep better after some time with a book, whether a detective story, an art dealer's catalogue, or a popular magazine. The important thing is a change of occupation. A round of golf or a few hands of bridge—and you are a new man.

*　*　*

Do not forget that the public is fickle, but rightly so. It does not need to be philanthropic and maintain artists who no longer bring it anything.

It has been said of this public that for years now we have been witnessing a world-wide standardization of its taste, that appetites, inclinations, and aesthetics have shown a strong tendency to become uniform. If this is true, is it a good thing or bad? Perhaps it is too early to judge. I leave this care to the critics, who should not be content merely with showing us the way, with warning us of the dangers of the road and the obstacles to avoid. They should instead be active catalysts in the world of music.

I ask nothing more of the critics. But this 'nothing' is still considerable. They should help us by pointing out the interesting young talents. A conductor does not have time to read through the thousands of new scores produced on the five continents each year or to attend every debutant's recital. But a good notice can point out the young performer who will be an interesting soloist in a year or two, bring to my attention the young composer whose first orchestral score I should watch for. Happy collaboration of this kind between critics and conductor can contribute a great deal to musical life.

On general principles I take a reserved attitude toward criticism. I know that, critic or conductor, man is not infallible.

It is not too bad to read in the papers from time to time that one is a blockhead, but if the gentlemen of the press feel free to say that what we are doing is terrible, they might at least take the trouble to let us know how they can tell. They do so only rarely, and I have the feeling they would be very much annoyed if we asked. I for one have been assassinated many times, but I am still among the living.

In any case, I have an absolutely inflexible rule never to retort to a criticism no matter how seriously it may seem to misrepresent the most obvious truth. No one ever wins an epistolary duel with the press.

* * *

In the end it is the public who writes our history, who names the masterpieces and the great interpreters—and it is hard to please. There is only one valid, certain, effective way to keep its favor: to practice our art with frankness and joy and to love music more than anything else in the world.

Appendix

THE REPERTOIRE
OF THE BOSTON SYMPHONY ORCHESTRA
IN ITS FIRST FIVE SEASONS
UNDER THE MUSICAL DIRECTION OF
CHARLES MUNCH

Titles marked with an asterisk were performed only by guest conductors.

Arbos. Tango*
Auber. La Muette de Portici. Overture
Bach, C. P. E. Symphony for String Orchestra No. 5
Bach, J. S. Das alte Jahr vergangen ist. Arr. by Charles
    Munch
    Brandenburg Concertos Nos. 1-6
    Cantatas Nos. 12*, 28*, 29 (Sinfonia), 50*, 80*, 83*, 93*,
        140*, 161*, 205
    Christmas Oratorio
    Concerto for Piano in D minor
    Concertos for Three Pianos in C and D minor
    Concerto for Piano, Violin, and Flute in A minor*

95

Concertos for Violin in A minor and E major*
Concerto for Two Violins
Die Kunst der Fuge. Arr. by Ernst Munch
Magnificat
Mass in B minor*
Musikalisches Opfer
Passacaglia and Fugue in C minor. Arr. by Respighi*
The Passion according to Saint John
The Passion according to Saint Matthew
Suites Nos. 1-4
Barber. Adagio for String Orchestra
The School for Scandal. Overture
Symphony No. 2*
Barraud. Le Mystère des saints innocents*
Bartók. Concerto for Orchestra*
Concerto for Viola*
Concerto for Violin*
Dance Suite*
The Miraculous Mandarin. Suite*
Music for Strings and Percussion
Two Pictures
Beethoven. Concertos for Piano Nos. 1, 2*, 3, 4, 5
Concerto for Violin
Coriolanus. Overture*
Egmont. Overture
Fidelio. Overture
Die Geschöpfe des Prometheus. Suite*
Gratulationsmenuette
Leonore. Overtures Nos. 2, 3
Missa Solemnis
String Quartet, Op. 131*
Symphonies Nos. 1-9
Berg. Der Wein*
Berger. Ideas of Order
Berlioz. Béatrice et Bénédict. Overture
Benvenuto Cellini. Overture
Le Corsair. Overture

La Damnation de Faust
L'Enfance du Christ
Harold en Italie
Les Nuits d'été
Requiem
Roméo et Juliette
Symphonie fantastique
Te Deum
Les Troyens. Chasse et orage
Bizet. Carmen. Excerpts*
Symphony
Bloch. Baal Shem
Concerto for Piano*
Concerto Grosso No. 2
Borodin. Prince Igor. Polovtzian Dances
Brahms. Concertos for Piano Nos. 1, 2
Concerto for Violin
Piano Quartet Op. 25. Arr. by Schoenberg*
Requiem
Symphonies Nos. 1-4
Tragic Overture
Variations on a Theme by Haydn
Britten. Variations on a Theme by Frank Bridge
Bruch. Concerto for Violin, No. 1
Bruckner. Symphony No. 7
Busoni. Berceuse élégiaque*
Chabrier. Bourrée fantasque
Joyeuse marche*
Chausson. Poème*
Symphony
Chavez. Sinfonia India*
Cherubini. Anacréon. Overture
Chopin. Concerto for Piano, No. 2*
Cimarosa. Il Matrimonio segreto. Overture*
Copland. Appalachian Spring
Concerto for Piano
Preamble*

97

Quiet City
Statements
Symphony No. 3*
Couperin. Concerto dans le goût théâtral. Arr. by
    Oubradous
    La Sultane. Overture and Allegro. Arr. by Milhaud*
Cowell. Hymn and Fuguing Tune No. 3*
Creston. Symphony No. 2*
Dallapiccola. Canti di prigionia*
Debussy. Épigraphes antiques. Arr. by Ansermet*
    Gigues*
    Ibéria
    Jeux*
    Le Martyre de Saint Sébastien. Excerpts*
    La Mer
    Nocturnes, Nos. 1, 2
    Prélude à l'après-midi d'un faune
    Printemps
Delius. Marche caprice*
    Summer Night on the River*
Diamond. Symphony No. 3
    Timon of Athens*
Dittersdorf. Symphony in C
Dukas. L'Apprenti sorcier
Dutilleux. Symphony
Dvorak. Concerto for Violoncello
    Symphonies Nos. 4, 5*
Elgar. Enigma Variations
de Falla. The Three-Cornered Hat. Three Dances*
Fauré. Ballade
    Dolly. Arr. by Rabaud
    Pélléas et Mélisande. Suite
    Pénélope. Prelude
Foss. Concerto for Piano No. 2
    A Parable of Death*
    The Prairie. Excerpts*

Song of Anguish*
Song of Songs*
Franck. Les Djinns*
   Psyché. Suite*
   La Rédemption. Symphonic Piece
   Symphony
Frescobaldi. Four Organ Pieces. Arr. by Ghedini*
Gabrieli, A. La Battaglia. Arr. by Ghedini*
Gabrieli, G. Sonata pian e forte
Gershwin. Rhapsody in Blue*
Ghedini. Architetture
   Pezzo concertante*
Gluck. Alceste. Divinités du Styx*
   Alceste. Overture
   Orfeo ed Euridice. Che farò senza Euridice*
Gould. Spirituals*
Grieg. Spring*
Haieff. Concerto for Piano
Handel. Concertos for Organ, Nos. 10, 13
   Concerto for Viola. Arr. by Casadesus
   Concerti grossi, Op. 6, Nos. 4, 10
   Concerto Grosso for Two Wind Choirs and Strings in F
   Fireworks Music. Suite
   Il Pastor fido. Suite*
   Water Music. Suite
Harris. Kentucky Spring*
Harsanyi. Symphony in C
Haydn. Concerto for Organ in C
   Concerto for Piano in D
   Concerto for Violoncello
   L'Isola disabitata. Overture
   Nelson Mass *
   Sinfonia concertante, Op. 84
   Symphonies Nos. 86, 88, 92, 93*, 95, 99, 100, 101, 103, 104
   Theresa Mass*

Hindemith. Concerto for Organ, Op. 46, No. 2
   Mathis der Maler. Symphony*
   Nobilissima Visione*
   Symphonic Dances*
   Symphonic Metamorphoses of Themes by Weber
Honegger. La Danse des morts
   Jeanne d'Arc au bûcher
   Monopartita*
   Pacific 2-3-1*
   Prelude, Fugue, and Postlude
   Symphonies Nos. 1, 2, 5
Ibert. Concerto for Flute
   Escales*
d'Indy. Fervaal. Introduction
   Symphony No. 2
   Symphony on a Mountain Air
Jolivet. Concerto for Ondes Martenot
Kabalevsky. Concerto for Violoncello
Khachaturian. Concerto for Violin*
Klami. Vipusessa Käynti*
Lalande. De Profundis*
Lalo. Concerto for Violoncello
   Le Roi d'Ys. Overture
   Symphonie espagnole
Liszt. A Faust Symphony
   Les Préludes*
Lopatnikoff. Divertimento
Madetoja. Sammon Ryöstö*
Mahler. Das Lied von der Erde*
   Lieder eines fahrenden Gesellen*
   Symphonies Nos. 2*, 4*, 5*, 9*, 10 (Adagio)*
Martin. Concerto for Seven Wind Instruments*
Martinu. Concerto for Piano No. 3
   Symphony No. 1
Mendelssohn. Concerto for Piano No. 1*
   Concerto for Violin
   The Hebrides. Overture*

APPENDIX

A Midsummer Night's Dream. Overture
Symphonies Nos. 3*, 4, 5
Mennin. Symphony No. 5
Messiaen. Turangalîla*
Milhaud. Concerto for Piano No. 4
Concerto for Violoncello No. 1
La Création du monde
Introduction and Funeral March*
Kentuckiana*
Suite Concertante for Piano and Orchestra
Suite No. 2*
Symphony No. 1*
Mozart. Adagio and Fugue, K. 546
Concertos for Piano, K. 271*, 414*, 450*, 456*, 467
Concerto for Two Pianos, K. 365*
Concertos for Violin, K. 216, 219, 271A
Così fan tutte. Per pietà
Divertimentos, K. 136, 287
Die Entführung aus dem Serail. Overture*
Idomeneo. Excerpts*
Litaniae, K. 125*
Masonic Funeral Music, K. 477
Missa Brevis, K. 192*
Le Nozze di Figaro. Overture
Le Nozze di Figaro. Deh vieni non tardar
Serenades, K. 250*, 361, 388, 525
Symphonie Concertante, K. 364
Symphonies K. 297, 319*, 338*, 385, 504, 543, 550, 551
Musorgsky. Khovanshchina. Prelude*
Night on Bald Mountain*
Pictures at an Exhibition. Arr. by Ravel*
Nabokov. La Vita nuova
Nielsen. Symphony No. 5
Paganini. Concerto for Violin, No. 1
Pfitzner. Palestrina. Three Preludes
Pijper. Symphony No. 3*
Piston. Fantasy for English Horn, Harp, and Strings

Suite No. 2
Symphony No. 4
Toccata
Poulenc. Concerto for Piano
Prokofieff. Chout. Suite*
  Classical Symphony
  Concertos for Piano Nos. 2*, 3*
  The Love for Three Oranges. Scherzo and March
  Symphonies Nos. 5*, 6, 7
Purcell. Four Fantasies
Rabaud. La Procession nocturne
Rachmaninoff. Concertos for Piano Nos. 2, 3*
Rameau. Dardanus. Suite
Ravel. Alborada del gracioso*
  Bolero
  Concerto for Piano
  Concerto for Piano, Left Hand
  Daphnis et Chloé. Suites Nos. 1, 2
  Don Quichotte à Dulcinée
  Ma mère l'oye*
  Pavane pour une infante défunte
  Rapsodie espagnole
  Shéhérazade
  Le Tombeau de Couperin
  Tzigane*
  La Valse
  Valses nobles et sentimentales
Read. The Temptation of Saint Anthony*
Reger. Romantische Suite *
Respighi. The Pines of Rome*
Rimsky-Korsakov. Le Coq d'or. Suite*
Rivier. Concerto for Violin
Rossini. La Gazza ladra. Overture*
  L'Italiana in Algerì. Overture*
  La Scala di seta. Overture*
  Semiramide. Overture*
Roussel. Bacchus et Ariane. Suite No. 2

Concerto for Piano
Le Festin de l'araignée
Symphonies Nos. 3, 4
Saint-Saëns. Concerto for Piano No. 3
   Concerto for Violin No. 3
   La Princesse jaune. Overture
   Symphony No. 3
Samazeuilh. Nuit
Schoenberg. Kammersymphonie
   Music to Accompany a Cinema Scene*
Schubert. Mass No. 2
   Rosamunde. Excerpts
   Symphonies Nos. 2, 4, 5, 7, 8
Schuman. Concerto for Violin
   Symphony No. 3*
Schumann. Concerto for Piano
   Concerto for Violoncello
   Genoveva. Overture
   Manfred. Overture
   Symphonies Nos. 1, 2, 4
Scriabin. Le Poème d'extase*
Shapero. Symphony (Adagietto)*
Shostakovich. Symphonies Nos. 1*, 5*
Sibelius. Finlandia
   The Origin of Fire*
   Pohjola's Daughter*
   Symphonies Nos. 1*, 2*, 4*, 5*, 6*
Smetana. The Bartered Bride. Overture
Smit. The Parcae. Overture
Strauss. Le Bourgeois gentilhomme*
   Divertimento (after Couperin)
   Don Juan
   Don Quixote
   Ein Heldenleben*
   Der Rosenkavalier. Suite*
   Symphonia Domestica
   Till Eulenspiegel*

Tod und Verklärung
Stravinsky. Le Baiser de la fée. Divertimento*
    Danses concertantes*
    Jeu de cartes
    Oedipus Rex*
    L'Oiseau de feu. Suite*
    Petrouchka*
    Pulcinella*
    Le Sacre du printemps*
Swanson. Short Symphony
Tchaikovsky. Capriccio Italien*
    Concerto for Piano No. 1
    Concerto for Violin
    Romeo and Juliet
    Symphonies Nos. 4, 5*, 6
Tcherepnin. Concerto for Piano No. 2
Thompson. Symphony No. 3
Thomson. Louisiana Story. Suite*
Toch. Symphony No. 2
Vaughan Williams. Concerto for Two Pianos
    Fantasia on a Theme by Thomas Tallis*
    Fantasia on the Old 104th Psalm Tune*
Villa-Lobos. Choros No. 10*
Vivaldi. Concerto grosso Op. 3, No. 11
Wagenaar. Symphony No. 4*
Wagner. A Faust Overture
    Der fliegende Holländer. Overture*
    Götterdämmerung. Excerpts
    Die Meistersinger. Excerpts
    Parsifal. Excerpts
    Siegfried Idyll
    Tannhäuser. Overture
    Tristan und Isolde. Prelude and Love-death
    Die Walküre. Excerpts
Walton. Symphony
Weber. Euryanthe. Overture
    Der Freischütz. Overture
    Oberon. Overture